The Natural History of
AGGRESSION

Chairmen of the Sessions

G. E. BLACKMAN, F.R.S., President of the Institute

JOHN BOWLBY, M.D.

Sɪʀ JULIAN HUXLEY, F.R.S.

Sɪʀ SOLLY ZUCKERMAN, C.B., F.R.S.

INSTITUTE OF BIOLOGY SYMPOSIA NO. 13

The Natural History of

AGGRESSION

Proceedings of a Symposium held at the British Museum
(Natural History), London, from 21 to 22 October 1963

Edited by

J. D. CARTHY

Department of Zoology, Queen Mary College, London

and

F. J. EBLING

Department of Zoology, University of Sheffield

Published for the Institute of Biology by

1964

ACADEMIC PRESS

LONDON AND NEW YORK

ACADEMIC PRESS INC. (LONDON) LTD
Berkeley Square House
Berkeley Square
London, W.1

U.S. Edition published by
ACADEMIC PRESS INC.
111 Fifth Avenue
New York 10003, New York

Library of Congress Catalog Card Number: 64-8369

PRINTED IN GREAT BRITAIN BY
A. QUICK & CO. (PRINTERS) LTD., OXFORD ROAD, CLACTON-ON-SEA

CONTRIBUTORS

Stanislav Andreski, *Department of Sociology, University of Reading, England* (p. 129)

John Burton, *University College, London, England* (p. 145)

J. D. Carthy, *Department of Zoology, Queen Mary College, London, England* (p. 1)

F. J. Ebling, *Department of Zoology, University of Sheffield, England* (p. 1)

James Fisher, *Ashton, Northampton, England* (p. 7)

Derek Freeman, *Institute of Advanced Studies, Australian National University, Canberra, Australia* (p. 109)

K. R. L. Hall, *University of Bristol, England* (p. 51)

L. Harrison Matthews, *Zoological Society of London, England* (p. 23)

Denis Hill, *Middlesex Hospital Medical School, London, England* (p. 91)

Arnold Klopper, *Obstetric Medicine Research Unit (M.R.C.), University of Aberdeen, Scotland* (p. 65)

James Laver, *formerly Keeper of Prints and Drawings, Victoria and Albert Museum, London, England* (p. 101)

Konrad Lorenz, *Max-Planck Institut für Verhaltensphysiologie, Seewiesen, Germany* (p. 39)

Cecily de Monchaux, *Psychology Department, University College, London, England* (p. 83)

Anthony Storr, *116 Harley Street, London, England* (p. 137)

Thelma Veness, *Psychology Department, Birkbeck College, London, England* (p. 77)

D. I. Wallis, *University of Aberdeen, Scotland* (p. 15)

PARTICIPANTS IN THE DISCUSSIONS

I. Berg, 49 *Hallam Street, London*

A. G. Bourne, 3 *Juniper Way, Tilehurst, Reading, Berks., England*

P. L. Broadhurst, *Department of Anatomy, University of Birmingham, England*

M. R. A. Chance, *Uffculme Clinic, Birmingham, England*

N. Cohn, 61 *New End, London*

E. H. Croft, 63 *Cookridge Avenue Cookridge, Leeds, England*

J. M. Cullen, *Department of Zoology, University Museum, Oxford, England*

C. J. O. Harrison, *British Museum (Natural History), London*

Sir Julian Huxley, 31 *Pond Street, London*

H. Kalmus, *Galton Laboratory, University College, London*

W. Lane-Petter, *Laboratory Animals Centre, M.R.C. Laboratories, Carshalton, Surrey, England*

D. Morris, *Zoological Society of London, England*

K. P. Oakley, *British Museum (Natural History), London*

W. M. S. Russell, 43 *Palace Court, London*

M. E. Solomon, *A.R.C. Pest Infestation Laboratory, Slough, England*

D. W. Tarry, 58 *Forest Road, Kew Gardens, Richmond, Surrey, England*

Marion A. Watson, *Rothamsted Experimental Station, Harpenden, Herts., England*

Anabel Williams-Ellis, *Plas Brondanw, Penrhyndeudraeth, Merioneth, Wales*

CONTENTS

PROLOGUE AND EPILOGUE

"THE question of questions for mankind" wrote Thomas Henry Huxley a hundred years ago, "—the problem which underlies all others, and is more interesting than any other—is the ascertainment of the place which man occupies in nature and of his relation to the universe of things." Zoologists are not ashamed that their discipline still embodies such a humanistic tradition. One value of biological studies is that they provide scale and perspective against which the origin, history and future of man may be viewed; another is that human anatomy, physiology and the neurological aspects of behaviour have been illuminated by comparative work on animals.

In one field, however, that of social behaviour, the comparative approach has developed more slowly. If, on the one hand, theologians and historians have regarded any admission of identity between human and animal behaviour as the final assault on the dignity of man, biologists—for a different reason—have been equally reluctant to make the comparison. To think of animal behaviour in terms of human drives, desires and goals was considered a dangerous and irrelevant exercise in anthropomorphic thought. Thus while the behaviourists amused themselves describing the tropisms and taxes of animals in semantically exact and sometimes utterly sterile scientific terminology, the psychologists were advancing ever deeper into the splendid chasms of the human mind by the manipulation of seemingly imponderable symbols created out of myth and dream. This now is history. Though animal psychologists appear to engage in constant re-appraisal of terminology, the application of psychological techniques to the study of animal behaviour no longer opens the zoologist to a charge of professional impropriety. Certainly the Institute of Biology had no inhibitions about inviting a group of biologists, psychologists, sociologists and historians to discuss the sources and significance of aggressive behaviour in animals and man.

We did not attempt to define "aggression", nor, with the exception of Veness, did our contributors. Nevertheless, at least in relation to aggression by individuals, it became clear that they were all talking about the same thing. An animal acts aggressively when it inflicts, attempts to inflict, or threatens to inflict damage on another animal. The act is accompanied by recognizable behavioural symptoms and definable physiological changes. We accepted the psychiatrists' view that in man, self-damage, perhaps nail-biting but certainly suicide, were analogous forms of behaviour—aggression directed inwardly. Similarly, aggression may be displaced towards non-human or inanimate objects, as when a child smashes a toy in a fit of pique or a man kicks his dog. It should be recognized that it is not the dog that the master seeks to injure; his aggression is directed towards what he recognizes as human in an animal which he addresses by name and abuses in words. No feeling of aggression need be aroused or satisfied by the act of killing a domestic chicken.

Except for the relationship of predator to prey, animals rarely destroy members of other species. Contributors are in common agreement that predation should not come within the scope of aggressive activity. The behavioural patterns and processes are not analogous; a hawk swooping on a small bird is no more aggressive than the family butcher engaged in his livelihood. Within these definitions aggression would appear to be almost entirely intra-specific. But there are exceptions, as James Fisher shows. If predatory birds are not aggressively orientated towards their prey, the prey may not reciprocate this attitude; crows mob eagle owls and small birds demonstrate noisily against cuckoos. But the most interesting examples of interspecific aggression amongst birds appear to arise as an "overspill" of an intraspecific aggressive drive. Such intraspecific aggression plays an important role in the maintenance of territory and is released by particular features such as recognition marks on the body of the enemy. Thus robins will not only attack other robins, but species of similar appearance as the red crossbill; what appears to be interspecific aggression is due to mistaken identity. On the other hand, very small taxonomic differences between related species may themselves act as releasers of aggression. There are, amongst birds, many groups of closely related sub-species, capable of interbreeding but not doing so, which have arisen as a result of geographical isolation. Birds of different sub-species are mutually intolerant when their territories come to overlap. Can there be, asks Fisher, an analogous situation amongst the races of man? Certainly Fisher's conclusions suggest an interesting paradox which remains substantiated in subsequent contributions. Aggressive orientation involves a recognition of similarity in the enemy, but at the same time aggression may be released by minor differences. The situation is well illustrated by recent skirmishes between groups of adolescents, known as "mods" and "rockers" at British seaside resorts.

Aggressive encounters between members of the same species occur in most vertebrates and in many invertebrates. According to Lorenz: if we put together two sticklebacks, lizards, robins, rats, monkeys or boys, who have not had previous experience of each other, they will fight; if we do the same with two animals of a different species, there will be peace—unless, of course, there is a predator-prey relationship between them. But it is clear from the contributions of Harrison Matthews, Lorenz and Hall that overt fighting to the death very rarely occurs in vertebrates, and it is doubtful whether it ever occurs in mammals under natural conditions.

Weapons such as teeth, claws, nasal horns and antlers would be very dangerous if turned against members of the same species; thus fighting is ritualized into display, threat, submission and appeasement, and such fights are no more than trials of strength followed by disengagement and rapid withdrawal by the weaker animals. Even in non-human primates, according to Hall, no group engages in fighting with other groups and real fighting within a group is of rare occurrence even in the most overtly aggressive species. True overt fighting in mammals only seems to occur when population numbers have overtaken the resources of the environment so that serious overcrowding is brought about.

Man appears to be an exception. The "unimagined strata of malignity in the human heart" have resulted, according to Freeman, in the death of 59,000,000 human beings from wars or other murderous quarrels between the years 1820 and 1945. Is human aggression innate? The current psychiatric evidence seems almost unequivocal; aggression is not merely a response to frustration, it is a deep-seated, universal drive. But is this part of the aetiology of war, and can the aggression of states in any sense be equated with the aggression of individuals? Agreement on the answer to this problem is not reached; indeed the very question appears to challenge the disciplinary frontiers of the sociologist and historian. Andreski, for example, says that there is no direct evidence which can throw light on the origin of war, but argues that human beings are not endowed with an innate proclivity for war; otherwise it would not be necessary to indoctrinate them to make them fight, and there would be no instance of nations remaining at peace for more than a generation. Norman Gibbs, who contributed to the symposium but could not offer a written contribution, was equally unable to bridge the gap between biologist and historian. Historians accept war as a component of human behaviour and analyse the causes of warfare between states in rational political and economic terms. Burton, too, rejects the whole notion of aggression by sovereign states, or at least takes the view that there is currently no evidence of such aggression. Whilst accepting that the notion of aggressiveness in animals may be valid, and accepting the psychologists' understanding of aggression in terms of frustration, fear, displacement, scapegoating and so on, he does not believe that human aggressiveness is thereby established as normal. Indeed, he takes the biologists and psychologists to task, both for asserting that there are aggressive tendencies amongst individuals and for implying that nation-states tend to act aggressively. This encourages every state to have an expectation of aggression, even though there is no discernable enemy, and the defence policy of the state will produce just the result it seeks to avoid.

The biologists clearly do not concur in this verdict, and their view is succinctly expressed in Lorenz's words. "There cannot be any doubt, in the opinion of any biologically-minded scientist that intraspecific aggression is, in Man, just as much of a spontaneous instinctive drive as in most other higher vertebrates. The beginning synthesis between the findings of ethology and psychoanalysis does not leave any doubt either, that what Sigmund Freud has called the 'death drive' is nothing else but the miscarrying of this instinct which, in itself, is as indispensable to survival as any other."

Even if no common agreement on the existence or nature of innate aggression amongst states is reached, it seems equally difficult to deny that there is any connexion between the causes and prosecution of wars and the subconscious springs of human aggression. Moreover, the terrifying history of overt aggression, of man's inhumanity to man, as catalogued by Freeman, cannot be refuted. It seems that man's destructiveness is essentially human. Animals display aggressive attitudes which may have a survival value, but under natural conditions they do not fight to the death with members of their own species; conflict is ritualized so that little damage is done. We are prompted, therefore, to ask certain questions. How far is man's aggressiveness, as displayed in war, subject to ritualization similar to that evolved by animals? If man's destructiveness is unique, why does he thus differ from other mammals? And finally, does the study of animal behaviour offer any hope that the "unimagined strata of malignity in the human heart" may be understood and overcome, so that men may live and evolve without fear of themselves?

If the prosecution of war has involved aggressive behaviour little short of genocide, the ritualistic aspects must also be admitted. Display and threat, the pomp and circumstance of glorious war, must throughout history have occupied at least as much military activity as actual conflict. Moreover, the posturing of politicians, the exchanges of notes, the delivery and rejection of ultimata, the declarations of war, the conduct of campaigns, the manoeuvring of troops and the techniques of combat all fall into clear, if continually changing, ritualistic patterns. Warfare may, as stated by Gibbs, have become more bloody with the spread of political democracy, but even total war has some—if few—redeeming features. It is not, as in the eighteenth century, possible for civilian tourists to travel without hindrance in enemy country. But, paradoxically, prisoners of war are, by international convention, entitled to certain courtesies according to their rank, even if their wives and children are simultaneously subject to calculated obliteration by aerial bombardment. The surrendering German generals after the battle of Stalingrad expected treatment as officers and gentlemen; their civilian masters were subsequently tried and hanged.

The destructive aspects of overt aggression, however, greatly outweigh the ritualistic in the human species, giving man an unenviable uniqueness amongst animals. Perhaps in the rapid development of weapons, by power of brain and hand, man's potentiality for destructiveness has far outstripped any inhibitions against fratricide or even genocide which might, as in carnivorous mammals, develop under the influence of natural selection. Perhaps the use of weapons at a distance could, in any event, vitiate such inhibitions; it may be psychologically easier to kill a man with a gun than with a knife, or to exterminate in mass by a hydrogen bomb than with a gas chamber. Or perhaps man is a prisoner within that unnatural environment which he has created for himself; holding all nature in subservience, his own position is analogous to animals living in overcrowded conditions or in captivity.

Can man learn to understand, ritualize or otherwise control his aggression when that aggression disrupts his society or leads to war? Even if states are not innately aggressive and war is not a direct consequence of subconscious aggressive drives, the prosecution of warfare releases aggression on a horrific scale. Can other outlets be found if we are mutually deterred to keep the peace? Perhaps as Storr suggests we may find substitutes in games, debates or the space race. We need more evidence. The techniques of sociological and psychiatric research might now be applied to direct observation of the aetiology of wars or of the tensions that lead to wars. International relations might be relieved of political emotions and objectively analysed in the light of psychoanalysis bearing the lessons of animal behaviour in mind. Humanity must, as Lorenz says, give up its self-conceit and accept that humility which is the prerequisite for recognizing the natural laws which govern the social behaviour of men.

J. D. CARTHY
F. J. EBLING
Symposium Convenors.

INTERSPECIFIC AGGRESSION

By

JAMES FISHER

Ashton, Northampton, England

CAIUS PLINIUS SECUNDUS, *alias* Pliny the elder, published his *Natural History* in about A.D. 77—two years before his death at Pompeii when prefect of Vespasian's fleet at Misenum. His knowledge of zoology has been underrated by many scholars: there is recent evidence, from late excavations, of a high standard of ornithology among the educated Pompeiians of his day, and I do not doubt that the good scholar was a member of the Campanian Ornithologists' Union, doubtless the President. Anyway he gives us an early, if not the earliest record of interspecific aggression unconnected with predation. Cuckoos, he wrote, "know how all birds hate them, for even the very smallest birds are ready to war with them".

The extent to which small birds, of the many species brood-parasitized by cuckoos, have developed the habit of mobbing them, has been elegantly demonstrated by Smith and Hosking (1955) in a series of observations and experiments. Such birds will react to cuckoos at all times, and will physically attack them, or stuffed mounts or models of them, when they have laid their first egg—the time when they are most likely to be parasitized. Placed at random in a wood, stuffed cuckoos attracted a demonstrating gang of garden warblers, nightingales, a blackcap, willow warblers, chaffinches, and a nuthatch, blue tit, coal tit and greenfinch. In spite of the close resemblance of cuckoos to sparrow hawks, these hawks elicited a quite different alarm and fear response from willow warblers, not involving aggressive postures. To the cuckoos, and particularly to their heads, the birds showed frenzied aggressive behaviour, and they extended this, interestingly, to mounts of the red-footed falcon which, unlike the sparrow hawk, has a head in shape and colour like that of the cuckoo; and towards a mount of the pallid cuckoo of Australia, a bird outside their range, smaller, with no bands on the breast but a similarly shaped head.

Apart from the birds already mentioned, cuckoos are mobbed and fiercely attacked when eggs are in the nest in western Europe and the Old World by many host birds, particularly meadow pipits; also by stonechats, sedge warblers, robins, whinchats, tree pipits, chiffchaffs, great reed warblers, red-backed shrikes, yellowhammers, woodlarks; but not by blackbirds (which are not parasitized by cuckoos) or hedge sparrows (which are regularly, and towards which no gens of cuckoo has produced a matching blue egg—an interesting exception to the general rule). Oropéndolas, which are very aggressive to the parasitic giant cowbirds of their own family, also react aggressively to large tyrant flycatchers which, though not brood parasites, compete with them for their own beautifully constructed suspended nests. Competition for nesting holes all over the world provokes much interspecific aggression and each woodland community has its own hierarchy of aggressive success among the competitors which include pigeons, woodpeckers, starlings, flycatchers, tits and sparrows in Europe.

In the Americas only one of the many cuckoos is parasitic; and none so in the United States. No small United States garden birds react to stuffed European cuckoos placed in their territories. On the other hand birds of the Americas will react violently to the various species of brood-parasitic cowbirds that use them as hosts, though in the winter some of the parasitized species may share vast roosts with their hosts.

I will pass quickly over the reactions of birds to predators, as the aggressive element in them must be familiar to anybody who has seen a group of mixed passerines mob an owl in daylight. Hartley (1950a) has made a good series of mount experiments with owls. So persistent is the drive to mob predators among some species that Thienemann noted wild crows visiting and aggressively demonstrating against a bough on which a captive eagle owl had been placed and mobbed, but from which it had been removed six months previously. The habit of mobbing predatory animals, particularly snakes, members of the weasel family, and both day-flying and night-flying raptors, and some predatory corvids, seems almost universal throughout the class of birds. Some species of owls have false eyes at the back of their heads, presumably an adaptation against such mobbing; though the very realistic false eyes on the back of the head of some kingfishers (including our common kingfisher) must be an adaptation not against this but attack by diurnal birds of prey when they are exposed on a riverside bough and concentrating on their fish watching.

Degrees of interspecific aggression are to be observed in practically all the maintenance and breeding activities of birds, particularly those that feed, roost or nest in mixed social groups. A commonplace of forests of all kinds from the tropics to the taiga is the presence of mixed flocks of opportunist foraging birds working through the canopy for insects or fruit; food which is often distributed in spots of local abundance—seasonal fruit bunches, the hibernacula of insects and the like—so that the discovery of one can be shared by all. Colquhoun (1942) found a hierarchy of aggressiveness, not unlike the intraspecific pecking order of a poultry yard, in the insect hunters of the English woods; with nuthatch at the top, great tit next, blue and marsh tits following in that order. These are birds which share the same ecology, at least for part of the year, and in so doing have evolved a privilege structure. Such structures are not unknown in mixed colonies of long-legged marsh birds—wood storks, ibises, herons and spoonbills; though they are rather rare in most sea birds, except perhaps the penguins in the great mixed colonies of the antarctic and sub-antarctic. Most sea-birds have evolved a refined nest site selection which on the whole prevents competition even in mixed colonies so crowded as those of the Pribilof or Funk Islands, Bear Island and St. Kilda. In the Atlantic, for instance, the puffin, Manx shearwater and Leach's petrel are burrow nesters, the storm petrel and razorbill crevice nesters, the gannet a broad ledge nester, the common guillemot a rock-top nester, which can be and is driven out from broad ledges by the gannet, the arctic guillemot a broad-top nester when alone, a small ledge nester when overlapping with the common guillemot, the kittiwake a small-ledge nester with a built up nest, the herring gull a top-slope nester, its sibling species the lesser blackback a sloping or even flat moorland nester near the cliff edge, the great blackback a hilltop nester near the highest points, the tystie or black guillemot a cliff-foot crevice nester. The fulmar prefers rather sheltered ledges but has more plasticity than the rest. The pattern is different in the Pacific, but with the accent on peculiar niches and some interesting differences; for instance the Pacific counterpart of the Atlantic puffin is not a burrow but a crevice nester, and the larger tufted puffin which has no Atlantic counterpart is a burrow nester. On the whole the seabird nexus is rather free from inter-specific strife; in some tropical parts of the oceans there is even some evidence that species with the same nest site preference breed at different seasons and thus avoid competition. Despite the scarcity of suitable land in some food-producing areas of the oceans, sea-birds have little significant nest site competition. All of which points to the generally accepted view that, setting aside predation and parasitism (and perhaps the special case of ants), birds and other animals are usually very tolerant of other species, even those that share part of their food spectrum. At least this is so in the wild: in captivity all sorts of extraordinary pecking-order interspecific hierarchies have been observed whose lessons are far from under-stood, except that zoo keepers have learned to think twice before they do such things as put drongos and honeyeaters in with other birds (they are formidably aggressive in confinement, as are even some hummingbirds) or put cranes, flamingos and pelicans together in too small an enclosure.

I must reach my point, if what I say is to have relevance to the main subject of this symposium. I am speaking purely as an ornith-ologist, who, some years ago regained his amateur status, but is still in touch with some of the literature, has grown up with the territory theory, and has literally or metaphorically sat at the feet of Huxley, Howard, Lorenz, Tinbergen, Armstrong and Hinde, and watched some of their powerful disciples attain equal status as prophets. There is now no argument about the universality of territoriality among birds, most other vertebrate animals, and a formidable galaxy of invertebrates. Intraspecific aggression has been recognized since Aristotelian times: it is now accepted as of such biological importance that out of a hundred chapters in vertebrate species monographs that I scanned at random, no less than twenty-two were devoted wholly or mainly to it.

Intraspecific aggression, it is generally agreed, takes place. What I am concerned with here is its overspill. Perhaps this is too trivial a word for the interspecific aggression that seems to stem, in the evolutionary sense, from intraspecific territorial behaviour. This appears to me to be of two main kinds, which I shall call hypersthenic, based on a surplus of drive, and in its most usual form involving mistaken identity or what looks like it; and taxogenic, that with potential as an evolutionary mechanism.

Many examples of the first kind of aggression have been collected by Armstrong (1947) and examples of what I believe to be the other by Wynne-Edwards in his important *Animal dispersion in relation to social behaviour* (1962). When we consider that the releaser or releasers of intraspecific fighting behaviour may be a particular part or parts—head, breast or some part of the body exhibiting a flash mark—we can easily understand how a robin can come to attack a red crossbill, or a goldfinch with its red face; or a bullfinch attack a reed bunting when the cock of this species has the black head of full breeding plumage, or an indigo bunting can scalp a painted bunting, which like it has a blue head. In some cases the displaying birds reach such a frenzy that the mistakes may be, to say the least, curious; Selous, as Armstrong quotes, saw a cock lapwing make a scrape before three stock doves and then, suddenly realizing his error, stop "with a little start". Thirty years ago, after his well-known field work on breeding birds in Greenland, Tinbergen (1935, 1936) became convinced that many interspecific demonstrations were the consequence of strong sexual desire influencing the power of discrimination of the territory owner.

The capercaillie is famous for its nuptial territoriality and oblivious concentration upon display at the onset of the breeding season: this trait permits it to be hunted easily in some countries with rather mediaeval game laws, and enabled Ferguson-Lees (1963) lately to report on five cock capers in Scotland that lived in small woods near roads and appeared to have no handy rivals of their own species; these drew the line at dogs, but they attacked sheep, a horse, people and motor cars; a case of overdrive, or hypersthenia, no doubt, and rather hard to categorize as a simple matter of mistaken identity.

Mayr's classical definitions of a species, now widely accepted by zoologists, or at least vertebrate zoologists, can be summarized thus. In 1940 he wrote that "species are groups of actually or potentially interbreeding natural populations, which are reproductively isolated from other such groups". In 1951 he added the refinement that species are also sufficiently ecologically specialized so as not to compete with others closely related to them (sibling species) in the same area. Mayr has established beyond reasonable doubt that the principal method of species formation is geographical, and not ecological isolation. Species arise when geographical subspecies or races, after a period of evolution in isolation, impinge upon the range of a neighbouring race. When this happens the two stocks may, although genetically different and statistically identifiable,* reintegrate, often with a period of much variation in the zone of overlap; or they may not. If they do not, speciation takes place, which means that each must have some mechanism for reproductive isolation, a preference for some different food spectrum, and probably also some concomitant differences in ecological requirements or preferences.

Rejungent taxa of this kind are so common that there are some scores of birds, out of the 8,500 or 8,600 species now living,† that are presently at the point of speciation, to the instruction and confusion of present avian taxonomists; though these share a remarkably unanimous view, nowadays, about species they are never likely to agree about the last 1 per cent: simply because evolution is a process, and not something that once happened.

Wynne-Edward's excellent, challenging and scholarly recent book lists many sibling species which show interspecific aggression. A classic case is that of the two north American meadowlarks investigated by Lanyon (1957). These icterids are outwardly almost identical, have some, but not complete ecological differentiation in regard to their habitats, and occupy a broad area of sympatry in the Middle West without interbreeding. In areas of mutual ecological suitability they behave territorially to each other as to their own kind, with similar or identical displays; and their most overt difference lies in their song, a difference which is great, and which permits the bird watcher to heave a sigh of relief, for the plumage differences are elusive in poor light. The song difference is doubtless a principal, if not the principal, isolative mechanism. The territorial aggression seems, at what must be a very early stage of their speciation, an essential also.

Wynne-Edwards quotes this, and other cases, particularly a group of sibling wheatears (Hartley, 1949, 1950 a, b; Simmons, 1957), in support of his refutation of Gause's principle (1934), that no two close species with a similar, or the same, ecology can live in the same area. I do not believe that this can yet be accepted, for every

*To the extent that, in regard to one or more characters which for practical purposes must be identifiable in a museum, 75 per cent of one population differs significantly from 98 per cent of the other: a practical yardstick for valid races in use since Amadon (1949).
†8,580 by a recent count of the writer's.

speciation has its transition stage. Speciating birds are now being quite often caught in the act. Moreover an ecological similarity may be great in certain places or at certain times of year, but lesser in the whole view. Most of the sibling wheatears he quotes with apparently the same ecology and interspecific aggression had their territorial systems only in the winter quarters.

It must be stressed that for rejungent taxa (I say taxa deliberately rather than races of species), to succeed in speciation a *complete* pre-adaptation with isolating mechanisms and compatible ecological habits is not necessary. It is for pre-adaptation to insert the end of the wedge, which becomes broadened by further isolating mechanisms and ecological compatibility factors (as Mayr calls them) by natural selection after the overlap. Not until *full* ecological differentiation has been reached, and full recognition devices of plumage or song or both become developed, can most siblings coexist with overlapping territories, and finally dispense with interspecific territorialism. Our own close sibling chiffchaffs and willow warblers seem to be in an intermediate stage; their territories can physically overlap where their rather different habitats abut, but they still show some degree of mutual intolerance. Territorial aggression, in so far as it is directed at a rejungent sibling, must be favoured by natural selection in the early "geological life" of a species, especially when both siblings still share some broadish bands in the food spectrum. It is at this time of taxogenic significance.

This is the point where, I am forced to say, the amateur ornithologist and quondam medical student treads warily. I suspect that this symposium (and I note with some satisfaction that our agenda ultimately provides for a literal interpretation of the word) has been gathered with a rather Martian eye on one particular mammalian species. Considering the fate of mammals in the Pleistocene period I must say that *Homo sapiens* has done rather well. If we accept the general view of the senior paleontologists that the Villefranchian and the Blancan be admitted unto the Pleistocene, then the Pleistocene has lasted about 2 million years. During this time there has been about a baker's dozen of glaciations and subglaciations, with interglacials and interstadials between, which does not seem to have happened to our planet—a series of ice ages, I mean—since our galaxy, the Milky Way, last completed a revolution rather over 200 million years ago. It may well go on, for another 10 million years or more. So far the score is interesting from the evolutionary point of view. The two dominant vertebrate classes, mammals and birds, have taken a lot of punishment, as have the flowering plants. During the Pleistocene, from 2 million to ± 10 thousand years ago, the expectation of geological life of a bird species has gone down from about $1\frac{1}{2}$ million to about 40 thousand years; that of a mammal species from about $\frac{1}{2}$ million to about 20 thousand years. *Homo sapiens*, from the geological evidence and the dating by astronomical correlates (for that is what we have to go on; potassium/argon cannot measure so short, nor carbon fourteen so long), may be about 400 thousand years old, if Swanscombe man was one of us.

From the Martian point of view, which for my purposes of argument resembles a systematic ornithologist's view of a bird, and is conducted according to the rules of ordinary systematics, man is an old species with an history of classic subspecific differentiation. Many subspecies or races (and I say races here to mean subspecies under the ordinary rules) have been described and named. Those that seem valid, by ornithological or Martian standards, are often called subgroups by modern anthropologists; probably because the word race, as applied to man, now has a doubtful semantic sense. But if men were birds, the latest check list would separately and trinomially name what some now call Caucasoids, Negroids, probably also Capoids and Mongoloids, certainly also Australoids.* These are (or at least some until very recently were) valid taxa; and they have been slowly rejungent only since the end of the Stone Age; and as everybody knows the Stone Age ended at different times in different places, and still goes on in a few.

Until the very recent years of dispersive, colonial civilization the human species seems to have enjoyed the classic pattern of distribution of a successful mammal, with up to half a dozen valid geographical races, within many of which the paleontologists have found evidence of clinal trends—all standard textbook stuff. Puzzles that still present themselves are also classical: was *Homo neanderthalensis* a good species for instance? Might man have had a polyphyletic origin? Were there times and places of rejungence in the palaeo-history of his races? What happened then? The Skhul fossils in Asia Minor alone demonstrate the necessity for the paleontologists to keep on digging.

Re-reading one of Julian Huxley's most stimulating essays published in 1941, I find an optimism typical of its time but perhaps unjustified in view of events as they have unfolded in the last couple of decades. "Human evolution", he wrote, "is reticulate"; this in contrast to the general divergence of the evolution of other animals. "In man", he went on, "after incipient divergence, the branches have come together again, and have generated new diversity from their Mendelian re-combinations, this process being repeated until the course of human descent is like a network". Within the geographical scope of Russia, Europe and North America this of course was true, long before Hitler attempted to write the Aryan myth in blood across his maniacal European constitution. But globally reticulate? In South and Central America to a large extent. In Africa to some

---

* An up-to-date scholar's judgement (Cole, 1963) runs as follows:" If we were to attempt to classify man according to this rule (the 75 per cent rule, p. 11. fn.) —*which in fact is not done* (my italics)—we should be left with three sub-species: the Caucasoids (Whites or Europeans), the Mongoloids (Asians) and the Negroids (Blacks or Africans)." Cole would place the Australoids as "archaic White", and generally lump Capoids with Negroids.

extent, though in most areas not. In Australia insignificantly; in Europe and New Zealand scarcely, in North America and Asia to a slight extent (though Asia shows a rather clinal pattern from west to east). The races of mankind have not come together again, genetically, to an extent much more than enough to prove at least that they can. On the contrary, members of each major race, confronted severally with new liberties and new restrictions, new challenges and new problems, have indifferently produced upon each confrontation a taxogenic syndrome. Whatever their race, state of culture, education, democracy or political system, humans are behaving like birds, from Bulgaria to Alabama, Tanganyika to Indonesia, Notting Hill to the Republic of South Africa (where an almost textbook model caricature of speciation is being contrived). Paradoxically, I believe that racial aggression can only be destroyed by racial prides. Separate development, or whatever the South Africans now call it, will not work; it cannot work. It stems from racial hatred and racial fear: drives which I suggest are doubtless innate, but as doubtless conquerable by research, wisdom, teaching and the scorning of euphemisms, just as other inheritances—literal inheritances—from our past are slowly being conquered.

References

Amadon, Dean. 1949. "The Seventy-five Per Cent Rule for Subspecies." *Condor*, **51**, 250-258.
Armstrong, E. A. 1947. *Bird Display and Behaviour*. London: Lindsay Drummond, 431 pp.
Cole, Sonia. 1963. *Races of Man*. London: British Museum (Nat. Hist.), 131 pp.
Colquhoun, M. K. 1952. "Notes on the Social Behaviour of Blue Tits." *Brit. Birds*, **35**, 234-240.
F[erguson]-L[ees], I. J. 1963. "Studies of an Aggressive Capercaillie." *Brit. Birds*, **56**, 19-22.
Gause, G. F. 1934. *The Struggle for Existence*. Baltimore, Md.: Williams and Wilkins Co., 163 pp.
Hartley, P. H. T. 1949. "The Biology of the Mourning Chat in Winter Quarters." *Ibis*, **91**, 393-412.
Hartley, P. H. T. 1950a. "An Experimental Analysis of Interspecific Recognition." *Symposia Soc. exper. Biol. Cambridge*, No. 4, 313-336.
Hartley, P. H. T. 1950b. "Interspecific Competition in Chats." *Ibis*, **92**, 482.
Lanyon, Wesley E. 1957. "The Comparative Biology of the Meadowlarks (*Sturnella*) in Wisconsin." *Publ. Nuttall orn. Cl.*, No. 1, 67 pp.
Mayr, Ernst. 1940. "Speciation Phenomena in Birds." *Amer. Nat.*, **74**, 249-278.
Mayr, Ernst. 1951. "Speciation in Birds." *Int. Orn. Congr.*, **10**, 91-131.
Simmons, K. E. L. 1951. "Interspecific Territorialism." *Ibis*, **93**, 407-413.
Smith, Stuart, and Hosking, Eric. 1955. *Birds Fighting*. London: Faber and Faber Ltd., 128 pp.
Tinbergen, Niko. 1935. "Field Observations of East Greenland Birds. I: The Behaviour of the Red-necked Phalarope (*Phalaropus lobatus L.*) in Spring." *Ardea*, **24**, 1-42.
Tinbergen, Niko. 1936. "The Function of Sexual Fighting in Birds; and the Problems of the Origin of 'Territory'." *Bird Banding*, **7**, 1-8.
Wynne-Edwards, V. C. 1962. *Animal Dispersion in Relation to Social Behaviour*. Edinburgh and London: Oliver and Boyd, 653 pp.

AGGRESSION IN SOCIAL INSECTS

By

D. I. WALLIS

University of Aberdeen, Scotland

Introduction

BY definition, social insects are those which live together in colonies. Aggressive behaviour is part of the fundamental mechanism which maintains a colony as a separate entity. The colony is kept distinct from other colonies of the same and different species. Thus, aggression is primarily outwardly directed, i.e. extra-colonial. However, the extent to which aggression is inhibited between colony members does vary and examination of this aspect can help to elucidate the factors which normally evoke aggressive behaviour.

The functions of aggressive behaviour can be summarized as:
(*a*) an agent maintaining colony cohesion;
(*b*) an agent in intraspecific competition. A territory is often marked out by a particular colony, so ensuring colony cohesion, a food supply and a nest-site;
(*c*) in interspecific competition, which may again be for food-sources and nest-sites;
(*d*) in hunting behaviour. Some of the components of aggressive behaviour are shown in the killing of other insects, including ants, for prey.

The basis of colony distinctiveness and the reasons why aggression is primarily extra-colonial have long puzzled workers in the field and received much attention in the literature. In considering ants, bees and wasps, I shall survey, albeit briefly, three aspects of the subject: the components of aggressive behaviour; current views on the basis of colony distinctiveness; and the factors which influence aggression.

Components of Aggressive Behaviour

Examples from various species may be given. My own work on *Formica fusca* (Wallis, 1962a) illustrates the components of aggressive ponents seem to be shown by most social insects.

In *fusca*, aggression may consist of adoption of a "threat" posture, or of attack by "seizing" or "dragging". Seizing and dragging function to destroy or remove an alien ant from the nest. Seizing consists of gripping part of the attacked ant with the mandibles. Short, sharp rushes followed by seizing are often observed and puncture of the head or epinotum, or loss of a limb or antenna, may result. Dragging consists of seizing plus a locomotory element. The attacked ant is usually dragged out of the nest. In the threat posture, the head is raised and directed towards the other ant. The mandibles are held wide open with the labial mouthparts tightly withdrawn. Threat is classified as such because it is shown in association with seizing and dragging, and its components suggest it is an intention or incomplete seizing movement. Thus, when the reaction of a colony towards an alien is studied (Wallis, 1962b), it is found that as scores for seizing rise so do scores for threat. However, at the highest frequency of seizing, threat scores have started to decline. This and other evidence indicates that threat is shown most frequently at a moderate intensity of aggressive motivation.

When the response sequences of individuals are analysed, the frequency of transition from one response to another is a further way of demonstrating that responses are similarly motivated—Fig. 1. On the assumption that over short periods of time motivation does not alter greatly, responses linked by the highest transition frequencies are the expression of similar motivation. Fig. 1 supports

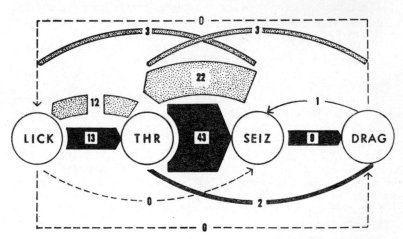

FIG. 1

The frequency of transitions from one response to another observed in ants encountering an alien. The thickness of the line and the figures indicate the frequency of the transition. Black indicates transitions in the direction of increasing aggressive motivation. Dashed lines show possible transitions which were not observed. THR=Threat.

the view that threat is linked with seizing. It suggests that licking (a response that will be considered later), threat, seizing and dragging, respectively, represent a gradual increase in a common motivation. Transitions from licking to dragging and vice versa are not observed, but dragging is most clearly associated with seizing, licking with threat. Significantly, dragging tends to show a negative rather than a positive correlation with threat when frequencies of the two responses are plotted against each other. Probably when dragging is evoked, motivation is so high as to inhibit a "low motivation" response such as threat.

Only two other responses are shown at all frequently towards alien ants—examining and licking. In "examining", the head and antennae are oriented towards another ant and may touch it. Information is probably obtained through the chemoreceptors on the antennae. "Licking" consists of cleaning another ant with the labial mouthparts. In part this serves merely to clean areas of an ant's body which it cannot clean for itself, but a more significant function is possibly that of removing exudates from the body surface which are the basis of the specific odour of the ant and of the colony. Much licking occurs of areas that the ant can clean for itself.

An aggressive response not seen in *fusca* is shown by *Formica rufa*. The gaster is brought forward between the legs and formic acid is squirted at an opponent. Many ants show a stinging response. In the evolution of the Hymenoptera, two trends are apparent. Some species possess a painful sting, e.g. honeybee, wasp, and some ants; a second trend has been towards the functional reduction and replacement of the sting by other defensive mechanisms, e.g. many ants including the genus *Formica*. The stinging response seems to be a high threshold one, only evoked at high levels of aggressive motivation.

Butler and Free (1952) have described aggressive behaviour in the honeybee. Bees show examining, licking, seizing, dragging and probably threat responses. A stinging response is shown. Bees, termed "guards", are frequently stationed at the nest entrance. They adopt a typical posture, frequently standing with forelegs off the ground and antennae held forwards. When more excited they open their mandibles—presumably this is equivalent to threat—and open their wings. Bees flying near the hive are watched carefully and bees landing are examined. If from another colony they are usually attacked. When fighting occurs, two bees often lie on their sides, holding on to one another's legs with their mandibles and attempting to sting each other. Often they buzz round and round extremely fast like a catherine wheel.

Bumblebees show similar behaviour. Free (1958) reports that guard bees are present, at least in large colonies. If the colony is disturbed, a guard may adopt a typical defensive posture by rolling over on to its side with the mid- and hind-legs of one side raised.

Sakagami (1960) describes the primitive social bee *Allodape* defending the nest entrance first by narrowing it with masticated pith and then by blocking it completely with the dorsal surface of the abdomen. Stinging is readily elicited. Similarly among Halictid bees, *Chloralictus* plugs the nest-entrance with her head. Michener and Lange (1958) report that guard bees back into the nest, where the tunnel diameter is greater, to allow nest-mates to enter. When an intruder appears, they may turn and block the entrance with the abdomen or they may face the intruder and show seizing. Disturbance of the nest may cause the bees to push dirt into the entrance and plug it.

Among wasps, Rau (1930) has described aggressive behaviour in *Polistes*. Surprisingly, some species of this genus show great tolerance towards workers from other colonies of the same species but attack workers of other species. Seizing, dragging, stinging and licking occur. Lin (1963) in describing the territorial behaviour of the cicada-killer wasp, *Sphecius speciosus*, gives an interesting account of the aggressive behaviour. The initial response is to fly straight at an intruder. "Threat" may be shown when the wasp gains on the intruder but then slows and returns to its territory. Increased aggressive motivation is reflected in the wasp "butting" the intruder and finally "grappling" with it. In grappling the wasp grasps the opponent only to separate almost immediately or falls to the ground and then separates. Loud buzzing is heard during grappling. Interestingly, only the males show this territorial aggressiveness.

The Basis of Colony Cohesion

A colony is maintained as a distinct unit because individuals are able to recognize colony members and differentiate them from non-colony members. The latter evoke aggressive behaviour. There seems little doubt that the basis of this colony distinctiveness is a specific colony odour, a conclusion supported by the work of McCook, Bethe and Fielde on ants and Kalmus and Ribbands (1952) on bees. There is little evidence that the odour is a result of definite secretions. It may be nothing more than odours absorbed selectively into the epicuticle. The origin of the odour has been the subject of controversy. Fielde (1904) concluded that colony odour is genetically controlled and, thus, a function of the foundress queen. She also postulated odour changes as a result of acquisition of new odours, presumably by surface adsorption. Her theories are complex and other authorities such as Wheeler have questioned them. On the other hand, Kalmus and Ribbands have shown that colony odour in bees is not wholly genetically controlled. Distinctive odours develop quickly if colony-halves receive different diets.

Normally, colony distinctiveness would result from differences in diet caused by colonies feeding on various crops in varying proportions. A similar non-hereditary mechanism might be expected in all social insects and some recent work of mine on ants attempted to investigate colony odour in this group (Wallis, 1962b). Three groups of about 50 *fusca* workers from the same colony were cultured separately. Groups A and B were fed on the normal culture diet; C was fed on black treacle. The odours of these foods are quite distinct (to man), much more so than the mixture of foods which two colonies might be expected to receive if they foraged naturally in different areas. The groups were kept in identical nests under the same conditions of light, temperature and humidity for seven months. Aggression shown by A to individuals of group C, to individuals of control group B, and, as a further control, to individuals from a different colony (X) was recorded. Colony X was fed like groups A and B. Results are given in Table 1.

TABLE 1. EFFECT OF DIFFERENTIAL FEEDING IN PRODUCING DISTINCT COLONY ODOURS

	n	Mean no. of aggr. responses	Significance	Lick	Threat	Seize	Drag
A against B	16	1·2 ⎫	P<0·05	5·6	1·1	0·1	0
A ,, C	16	3·5 ⎬	}P<0·001	9·9	3·2	0·3	0
A ,, X	16	19·7 ⎭		1·1	13·6	4·4	1·7
A ,, B				82%	16%	2%	0%
A ,, C		Percentages of total		74%	24%	2%	0%
A ,, X				5%	66%	21%	8%

A against B shows the aggression resulting simply from separation. In fact, an ant returning to its own colony often evokes slight aggression in ants guarding the nest entrance. The causes of this aggression, which is always much less than that shown to aliens, are discussed in the last section. The result of differential feeding (A against C) is to increase the aggression shown, since the mean number of aggressive responses rises from 1·2 to 3·5. Yet far greater aggression is shown towards alien ants from colony X. Further, proportionally more seizing and dragging is shown towards X. In fact, the response pattern to B and C ants is more like that shown towards returning nest-mates, where the commonest response is licking.

Thus, metabolic differences induced by different diets may play only a small role in producing distinct colony odours in ants, although more experiments need to be done on this question. Clearly, dietary differences can affect colony odour, but these results suggest genetic influences may be important. Possibly the mechanism in ants is somewhat different from that operating in bees.

Factors affecting Aggression: Apparent Breakdown of Colony Cohesion

Although alien colony odour is the principal stimulus evoking aggression in social insects, it is certainly not the only one. Visual cues may evoke aggression in bees, ants, and probably wasps. For example, the bobbing flight of bees about to rob another colony acts as a visual releaser and this is reinforced when the bee gets nearer by the alien odour releaser, as Free (1955) has shown. Dark colour or movement of any sort evoke more aggression in bees than light colours and still forms, according to Lecomte (1952). Tactile cues may be of some, but generally slight, importance. Free (1961) reports that stinging in bees is more readily evoked by rough than by smooth textures. Other chemical cues include formic acid which elicits attack in the ant *Camponotus* as Vowles (1952) has found, and the scent of mammals which Free (1961) states encourages stinging in the honeybee.

Other factors influencing the degree or type of aggression are territory, temperature, the degree of hunger and probably the presence of brood. In addition, my results show that different colonies, although cultured under the same conditions, may vary considerably in the amount of aggression they show to intruders (Wallis, 1962b). In any one colony, individuals vary in aggressiveness and the most active ants may also be the most belligerent.

Some observations on *Formica fusca* suggest that situation may be important in influencing aggression (Wallis, 1962b). Various results made it clear that an ant appearing at the nest entrance constituted a situation which alerted guard ants and might evoke aggression in them. Whether the ant is an alien or a nest-mate is clearly a separate factor and determines the subsequent response to the entering ant. Table 2 shows the response of a colony to entering ants. The entrants were either aliens or ants of the same colony which had been away from the colony (*a*) for 24 hours or (*b*) for less than a minute. Ants within the colony acted as controls to see whether any aggression is normally shown to ants within the nest.

TABLE 2. RESPONSE TO ALIENS AND NEST-MATES BY A COLONY

Ant towards which responses were made	n	Mean aggr. responses	Significance	Mean responses			
				Lick	Threat	Seize	Drag
A. Alien	15	15·5	A & B: P< ·001	8·3	13	2·4	0·1
B. Nest-mate away 24 hr.	15	5·4	B & C: Not sig.	9·8	5·2	0·2	0
C. Nest-mate away < 1 min.	20	4·1	C & D: P< ·001	6·2	4·0	0·1	0
D. Nest-mate within nest	10	0·1		0·1	0·1	0	0

What is surprising about these results is the amount of aggression evoked by ants returning to their own nests—an apparent breakdown in colony cohesion. Of course, the response pattern to aliens is different from that to returning nest-mates. Very little seizing and fewer threat responses are shown towards the latter, although they evoke a considerable amount of licking. However, some aggressive responses are evoked fairly consistently by ants returning to their own nests. Note that virtually no aggression is shown towards a nest-mate within the nest.

The length of time for which a nest-mate is away does not affect the aggression shown towards it. On the basis of odour alone, it seems doubtful whether there can be any odour difference between an ant within the nest and one which is away for less than a minute. The factor eliciting aggression in these circumstances seems to be the situation "ant-entering-the-nest". Foragers, too, evoke aggression on re-entering their nests. Aggression is shown on entry but not later. The factor here is one of orientation to a particular part of the nest. The entrance is probably detectable visually as an area of higher light intensity.

The association of licking with aggressive behaviour is interesting. Licking, as Table 2 shows, is rarely shown towards ants within the nest, but returning nest-mates are often licked for considerable periods. The mean duration of licking bouts shown towards returned nest-mates isolated for 24 hours is 30 seconds (n=147), but towards aliens is only $6\frac{1}{2}$ seconds (n=125). Response sequences show that licking tends to be linked with threat rather than with seizing or dragging. But licking and threat probably do not share causal factors to a great extent, for threat scores show a negative correlation with licking scores. Licking seems to be elicited by some of the factors evoking aggression, e.g. "ant-entering-nest", but also by other, quite different factors. Ants outside the nest would be likely to adsorb foreign odours on to their body surfaces and this odour difference may evoke both licking and aggression in other ants. The function of licking in this context may be to reincorporate a returned ant into the colony by removing any adventitious odours. Aggression shown towards a returned ant, on the other hand, tends to disrupt the colony. The fact that much licking and little aggression is shown towards returned nest-mates, but much aggression and less licking towards aliens, indicates that the total response pattern tends to reincorporate nest-mates but exclude aliens from the colony.

Colony odour seems to be learned by nest members. An individual seems to learn the collective odour of the colony by a rapid learning process similar to "imprinting" soon after emergence from the cocoon. Thus, pupae can be transferred to other nests and the adults which emerge show allegiance to the nest in which they find themselves. In this way, *fusca* slave-ants develop an allegiance to the *Formica sanguinea* colony into which they emerge. However, some experiments I did on the ant *Lasius flavus* suggest that some further learning of colony odour is possible, since one colony may be habituated to some extent to the odour of another, if exposed to an airstream which has passed through the other colony. Ants are probably continually habituating to the slight variations in the odour of their nest-mates. If an ant is separated from its nest-mates, the habituation decays and it may show a few aggressive responses itself when it returns to the nest. In very primitive ponerine ants, Haskins and Haskins (1950) found evidence that unless all members of a given community are in relatively continuous contact schisms will develop so that isolated colony-portions become permanently hostile to the rest. This may be due simply to a decay in habituation or to metabolic changes altering individual odours to which all ants would normally habituate.

Conclusion

In summary, it is clear that aggression is primarily channelled into extra-colonial encounters by the development of distinct colony odours, but that the complexity of the factors governing aggressiveness results in apparent exceptions to this. This complexity is the result of the nature of the colony odour itself with its probable tendency to vary with time and the likelihood of small differences occurring between individuals.

References

Butler, C. G., and Free, J. B. 1952. *Behaviour*, **4**, 262-292.
Fielde, A. 1904. *Biol. Bull.*, **7**, 227-250.
Free, J. B. 1955. *Behaviour*, **7**, 233-240.
Free, J. B. 1958. *Behaviour*, **12**, 233-242.
Free, J. B. 1961. *Anim. Behav.*, **9**, 193-196.
Haskins, C. P., and Haskins, E. F. 1950. *Ann. ent. Soc. Amer.*, **43**, 461-491.
Kalmus, H., and Ribbands, C. R. 1952. *Proc. Roy. Soc., Lond., B.*, **140**, 50-59.
Lecomte, J. 1952. *Behaviour*, **4**, 60-67.
Lin, N. 1963. *Behaviour*, **20**, 115-133.
Michener, C. D., and Lange, R. B. 1958. *Insectes Sociaux*, **5**, 379-401.
Rau, P. 1930 *J. compar. Psychol.* **10**, 267-286.
Sakagami, S. F. 1960. *Insectes Sociaux*, **7**, 231-249.
Vowles, D. M. 1952. *Adv. Sci.*, **10**, 18-21.
Wallis, D. I. 1962a. *Anim. Behav.*, **10**, 105-111.
Wallis, D. I. 1962b. *Anim. Behav.*, **10**, 267-274.

OVERT FIGHTING IN MAMMALS

By

L. HARRISON MATTHEWS

Zoological Society of London, England

INTRASPECIFIC fighting has been divided into two kinds, ritual and overt, the first a formalized sparring match with strict rules, the second a fight to the death with the gloves off and nothing barred. In preparing this paper the more I have sought examples of such intraspecific overt fighting in mammals the less I have succeeded, and I doubt that it normally occurs in nature.

Fighting needs weapons, and most mammals use their teeth and claws, structures that originally had other functions. Both teeth, primarily used for seizing food and reducing it to fragments, and claws, primarily a protection for the ends of the digits, are easily adapted as efficient weapons of aggression through a little emphasis on their size, shape, and sharpness. In many orders of mammals they are variously adapted as weapons, tools with many different uses, and, at least the teeth, even as sexual and status symbols.

Aggressive weapons that are neither teeth nor claws have been evolved in only a very few orders of mammals. Because one of these orders, the artiodactyles, is widely distributed and numerous in species we are inclined to think that special aggressive weapons are of widespread occurrence among the mammals. But are they? They are present in only three orders, the monotremes, the perissodactyles, and the artiodactyles. (Stink glands are so only interspecifically; intraspecifically they are scent glands. Spines and armour are defensive, not aggressive adaptations.) The male platypus and echidna have on the inner side of the ankle a spur connected with a "poison" gland. Among the perissodactyles the rhinoceroses have nasal horns, and among the artiodactyles the deer have antlers, and the cattle, sheep, goats, and antelopes have horns. These three orders have two characters in common—they have reduced dentition and, except the echidna, no effective claws.

The function of the monotreme spur, whether as weapon or sexual stimulant is unknown, so we cannot discuss it here. The feet of rhinoceroses, adapted for carrying great weight and protected by hoof-like nails, are not weapons. The African rhinoceroses, which have the largest nasal horns, have no incisor teeth whereas the Asiatic species, which have comparatively small horns, have incisors modified as tusks. In all species, however, the horn or horns seem to be used less as intraspecific weapons than as sexual stimulants in the rough horse-play of courtship behaviour. In all the artiodactyles except the pigs and hippopotamus the upper incisors are reduced or absent; in many the upper canines are small and the lower ones incisiform. The limbs, with digits reduced in number and highly specialized for running, are provided with hooves. It is the artiodactyles with deficient anterior dentition that possess antlers or horns; in those without special weapons such as the musk and water deer, the chevrotain and some others the upper canines are tusks large enough to project between the lips when the mouth is shut. The weapons of the camelids are the canines reinforced by the retained caniniform outer incisor of the upper jaw.

Weapons, other than teeth and claws, are thus uncommon among the mammals although the accident of the artiodactyles containing a great diversity of species gives the contrary impression at first sight. It might be suggested that the diversity is the result of efficient arming with special weapons, but that argument seems invalid in view of the much greater number of species among orders such as the bats or rodents which are armed with nothing more than teeth and claws.

The use of weapons in interspecific fighting is primarily for protection against predators or for the capture of prey, functions that are readily understandable as biologically advantageous to the species. But it is not easy to see how intraspecific strife can have any value; it might eliminate the weaker individuals but the hazards of the environment will do that without action within the species.

Indeed on examining intraspecific fighting more than superficially it is at once apparent that an important part of animal behaviour, at least in the mammals, is directed towards avoiding intraspecific fighting. The weapons are potentially so dangerous that fighting is ritualized into display, threat, and submission or appeasement, so that fights are generally no more than trials of strength followed by disengagement and rapid withdrawal by the weaker. This does not mean that fights never end fatally, for a threat that is never carried out loses its meaning, but fighting to the death rarely happens in the normal environment.

It is, indeed, very difficult to find any examples of true overt fighting resulting in the death of the loser among mammals under normal conditions in the wild. It occurs only when population numbers have overtaken the resources of the environment so that serious overcrowding is brought about. This produces a situation similar to that of animals in captivity where the environment is artificially restricted so that aggression is increased and any chance of escape from the aggressor is denied. In both situations the animals are living in a biologically unsound environment which inevitably distorts the normal patterns of social behaviour. Even in overcrowded conditions, as for example during a vole plague, when the crash comes the animals do not necessarily die as a consequence of intraspecific fighting but rather from a general condition of stress.

The hippopotamus provides an example of overcrowding leading to fatal fighting. Verheyen found that in the Upper Semliki between Lake Edward and the River Karurume, a distance of 32 kilometres, there was a minimum of 2,087 hippopotamuses, or an average of one hippo to every 15 metres, with a greatest concentration of one hippo to every 5 metres in the upper $5\frac{1}{2}$ kilometres. In these conditions each group of females and young is attended by up to six adult males of approximately equal social rank in the hierarchy, each dominant only in the neighbourhood of his own wallow in the river. The males maintain their territories and their social rank by threat and fighting, most commonly by threat alone followed by withdrawal of the weaker. Fighting in different degrees of severity occurs, and wounds that appear to be very severe are inflicted, but as Verheyen points out hippos are well adapted to fighting and its consequences by their very thick skin on the back, flanks, rump, and tail, and by the astonishing speed with which the wounds heal. Nevertheless, when overcrowded, fighting sometimes ends with the death of one combatant: Verheyen examined the bodies of five hippos thus killed during the period when he made his observations.

Among the ungulates, fighting between stags of the red deer has been studied by Fraser Darling (1937) who shows that the antlers are used for threat and for fierce sparring but that the death of the vanquished is uncommon. For instance he watched an old switch stag take possession of a group of twelve hinds; among them there were six young stags which the old one chased out of the group one by one. Not one of them stopped to contest the point. The stag herded the hinds to join with two other groups of nine and six near which two eight pointer stags were standing. "These two stags, which were fairly fresh and in fine fettle, took good care to keep out of the way of the old switch, and he took no notice of them." The two stags roared at each other and approached with heads lowered; "the stags took slow steps forward, then a quick run, and their antlers were together. . . . And now one of them side-stepped and lunged, but the other wheeled his hind end and met his opponent's antlers with his own. The point in all these fights is to lunge a broadside in the opponent's ribs, and to prevent this happening to oneself. Much of the fight therefore, consists of a shoving match, antlers to antlers. The stag which can shove the harder is usually the winner, his opponent retiring before he gets a broadside." Darling further states, "Their hurts in fight seem to be of small account and a fatality is rare. The incidence of fighting is much exaggerated in popular literature describing deer. There is more noise and show than real fight . . . only stags of equal merit fight each other. No stag will face another better than himself."

Darling makes a very interesting remark about deer confined in parks where their numbers reach a high artificial density. "There stags fight in season and out, and stags will kill calves and strange hinds under such conditions. In short, overcrowding results in anti-social behaviour which in itself is one type of check to the further increase of a cramped population."

Pedersen (1962) found that in Greenland in areas with large populations of musk ox many skirmishes could be seen in the spring but rarely decisive fights. Often the solitary bulls try their luck against the superior herd leaders, and generally they are chased off at the first encounter. If a bull in full vigour is separated from his herd he becomes very restless at the rutting season and tramps around looking for another. As soon as he scents one he approaches and challenges the owner who will not be chased away so that a more serious fight occurs, the animals charging each other head on and crashing their frontal shields together. Pedersen watched such a fight for half an hour until one of the bulls seemed to be weakening: "The last shock pushed it over on to its hindquarters, and while its adversary prepared for a new assault it got up, turned round, and fled. The other bull made a show of pursuing it, and then returned to the herd." Pedersen adds that sometimes one of the bulls is killed and that he had seen the skeleton of a musk ox that had died from a fracture of the frontal part of the skull, and says he had been told of two others. He concludes, "It is, however, only rarely that fights finish in this way."

These examples are typical of the fighting behaviour in all the horned ungulates, where the weapons may be used in real earnest interspecifically, particularly against predators, but intraspecifically only to maintain territory or social rank or both, and not usually for killing rivals.

Barnett includes some interesting observations on intraspecific fighting in his studies on social behaviour in wild rats. He was able to establish caged colonies of wild *Rattus norvegicus* in which there was little or no fighting unless a strange rat was introduced. Fighting is essentially territorial and depends upon one rat, especially an adult male, being in a familiar place and encountering a stranger. Combat consists of tooth-chattering, threat posturing, leaping over the stranger and biting him. Barnett states that the biting is a pain-causing action likely to evoke flight in the rat attacked, and that it did attempt to escape by climbing up the side of the cage. In the experiments, however, there was little opportunity for flight and invariably the attacked rat soon died. The cause of death was not, as might be expected, the wounds caused by biting for they were always superficial and slight; the animals died from internal stress produced by the impossibility of completing their normal pattern of behaviour by escaping from the aggressor.

Among the carnivora the pinnipedes are generally highly social and polygamous animals during the breeding season in which the bulls defend territories and maintain harems of cows. In a polygamous species in which the sex ratio at birth is approximately even there must be a large number of males superfluous to the breeding needs of the species. Among the pinnipedes the master bulls keep their places by fighting their rivals. In a rookery of elephant seals numerous bachelor bulls loiter on the outskirts of the harems and try to poach the outlying cows while the master bull's attention is engaged elsewhere, but they generally quickly retreat without waiting to fight if he makes a rush at them. A serious fight takes place only when a strange bull seriously challenges the master. The method of fighting is stereotyped; the bulls approach each other closely, rear up on the hinder part of the body to a height of eight or nine feet, inflate their trunks and open their mouths widely giving vent to loud belching roars. They then throw themselves forward upon each other trying to tear the opponent with the large upper canine teeth. The blows are generally taken on the sides of the neck which are much lacerated so that old bulls are covered with a mass of wrinkled scars. Sometimes the damage is more serious, as when eyes are burst or knocked out or trunks are torn open, but the elephant seal, like the hippopotamus, is well adapted to fighting and can take a lot of punishment without serious results. I have never seen or heard of well matched elephant seals killing each other; the fights though apparently furious do not last long and as soon as the vanquished breaks away the victor chases him only to the territory boundary before returning to his cows. Fighting on a much less intense level often occurs between younger bulls without harems, and although many scars result the contestants, which are not defending territories, do not appear to be in great earnest.

The grey seal has a similar social structure of territories and harems, but its fighting is much less spectacular. If a master bull can catch an interloper a fight follows in which the bulls bite and tear each others' necks, but an intruder seldom waits to fight and retreats when the bull in possession of territory hastens towards him.

In the walrus the canine teeth are enlarged as long external tusks which are used for helping to hoist the heavy animals on to floating ice or over rocks ashore, and for fighting. Lamont (1876) says that "walruses use their tusks against one another very much in the method that game cocks use their beaks. From the animal's unwieldy appearance and the position of his tusks one is apt to fancy that the latter can only be used in a stroke downwards but on the contrary they can turn their necks with great facility and quickness and can strike either upwards, downwards, or sideways with equal dexterity. I frequently observed them fighting with great ferocity on the ice and the skins of the old bulls which are light coloured and nearly devoid of hair, are often covered with scars and wounds received from these encounters." He does not, however, suggest that fighting results in more than superficial damage—the walrus, like other large animals, is pretty tough and ignores anything but a mortal wound.

The sea lions and fur seals also are tough hard-fighting pinnipedes, which defend territories and harems during the breeding season. Bull fur seals of the Pribilof Islands are large animals weighing three or four times as much as the cows. They come ashore on to the breeding beaches a week or more before the cows arrive, and while waiting for them they take up their territories. The best territories are near the water's edge, and the first comers are quickly challenged by later arrivals which try to drive them from their positions to the lower grade territories further up the shore. They are immensely strong animals and fight ferociously but, although they appear to inflict grievous wounds, the damage is generally superficial and it is the exception for one of the contestants to be killed. When the cows arrive the bulls with territories nearest the water get the first pick so that it is not until their harems become too large for effective supervision that the bulls holding the less valuable territories further inland receive the overflow. The heavily pregnant cows get very rough treatment from the bulls but they too are tough and can take it. In a few days they give birth to their pups and quickly become receptive to the bulls at their post partum oestrus.

Among the fissipede carnivores that are gregarious and have a highly evolved social structure, such as the wolf, fighting is so ritualized that it lies beyond the scope of this paper. Wolves are potentially so dangerous to each other that an elaborate chain of submissive reactions of increasing intensity culminating in the weaker contestant throwing itself on its back to expose all the vulnerable parts of the body defenceless to the superior who refrains from taking the advantage presented, ensures that intraspecific fighting does not end fatally.

Crowcroft (1957) found that the common shrew fully lives up to its reputation of being very quarrelsome. A shrew holds only a small territory consisting of little more than its nest, and forages over an extensive home range which overlaps those of its neighbours. When two foraging shrews blunder into each other through their limited powers of sight—they rely chiefly on their sense of touch—they scream shrilly, bite each other's tail and feet, and appear to be locked in mortal combat. Suddenly one breaks away, rears up, and throws itself on its back, showing the lighter colouring of the belly. Does the victor at this signal rush in and tear out the throat of his helpless rival? On the contrary it immediately turns tail and runs silently away. This pattern of aggressive behaviour is independent of sex and individual recognition, and ceases only during oestrus and copulation. Crowcroft points out that "the food of shrews is scattered about in tiny parcels" each of which must supply sufficient energy to keep the animal going long enough to find another. "The road to survival lies, not in hunting intensively through a patch of litter or soil for something which may not be there, but in rapidly and superficially inspecting many such patches. In a familiar area an animal learns the best places to find food and makes its way from one to another quickly and by safe routes." He concludes that the fighting of shrews is a mechanism which helps to separate animals whose feeding areas overlap, and which does so with the minimum expenditure of time and energy. It does not result in injury or death.

Work on the social structure of groups of several species of primates such as the pioneer studies of Zuckerman, has mostly been carried out on colonies in captivity. Similar work in the field, such as that of Goodall (1963) on chimpanzees and of Hall (1963) on baboons has shown that the social hierarchies in the natural environment are much less rigid than in the artificial one of captivity. In captivity the animals of lower social rank cannot avoid infringing the territories of their superiors so that there is much emotional arousal, continual displays of threat or submission, and frequent fights from which the weaker cannot escape. In the wild the animals do not live in this state of emotional tension, and although the dominant animal takes the first place he is not forced to be constantly holding his position by aggressive behaviour.

Goodall found that among groups of chimpanzees the dominant male tolerated the presence of other adult males, and that there is no fighting for food or females provided he is given precedence. The baboons studied in South Africa by Hall, on the other hand, lived in troops with only one dominant adult male, a number of females and young of both sexes. The subadult males when approaching maturity leave the troop. The baboon resembles the seals in being polygamous and in having an approximately even sex ratio at birth; a high proportion of the males must therefore be superfluous to the reproductive needs of the species. There is no evidence, however, that the dominant males fight with or kill these superfluous potential rivals, and at present nothing is known of what happens to them. In polygamous mammals nature seems to be as lavishly wasteful of male somatic cells as she is universally of male gametes.

Wood Jones describes fighting in some of the marsupials of South Australia when confined in captivity and he says: "Bandicoots are desperately pugnacious . . . their methods of fighting are peculiar. The aggressor will tirelessly follow his victim until he wears him down . . . when one animal overtakes the other and presses it to an engagement the assault is made by a jump and an endeavour to strike with the claws of the hind feet. Each stroke carried home removes some hair from the victim's back and scratches the thin skin. . . . They seem never to fight face to face for when the chase leads to such a meeting, one instantly jumps over the other inflicting a blow with the hind foot in passing and renews the attack from the rear. Only as a last resort, although the whole encounter has been conducted with open mouths, do they start to bite each other." . . . "Barred bandicoots (*Perameles*) become very tame and familiar in captivity but although they are extremely gentle when kept as pets, they are desperately pugnacious among themselves. On one occasion when eight live specimens were sent from Ooldea, all eight were dead and almost devoid of hair when they arrived in Adelaide. They had fought each other to the death on the railway journey . . . the fighting is done largely with the long feet."

Of the Nuyt's Islands bandicoot, *Isoodon nauticus*, Wood Jones says: "In captivity the island bandicoot displays habits exactly similar to those of its larger mainland relatives. . . . Owing to the density of the bandicoot population on the island, fights must be very frequent and only one specimen with a whole tail was captured; all other examples possessed nothing but mere stubs of varying length; ragged ears are also the rule." These injuries, however, do not tally with the method of fighting he describes, which is also found in the rat-kangaroo (*Bettongia*). "Even if kept in large runs when in captivity the males will fight to the death . . . one animal pursuing and scratching the fur from the other as it jumps over it. In this way the victim is worn out; and plucked of its fur and scored by deep furrows produced by its rival's strong claws, it dies of exhaustion."

By no means are all the marsupials so aggressive intraspecifically for in describing the habits of *Chaetocercus*, the crest-tailed pouched mouse, he tells how it kills mice and birds for food and adds: "Although such bloodthirsty little animals they do not quarrel among themselves and they may be placed together in a cage regardless of sex or acquaintance; in this respect they differ remarkably from several less carnivorous marsupials."

These Australian fighters are evidently strongly territorial so that they cannot tolerate the presence of an intruder. The fighting to the death described by Wood Jones took place when the animals were held in captivity in quarters too narrow to provide space for more than one territory. He does not suggest that fighting among these creatures when free has a similar result, and he tacitly admits as much in pointing out that the high density of the population of bandicoots on Nuyt's Island was the cause of fighting and mutilation.

All the examples of intraspecific fighting described in this brief survey show the impossibility of sharply separating overt from ritual fighting, for the two form a cline with very different ends joined by an unbroken line. Even in overt fighting the technique of the ring follows a stereotyped pattern with the result that a fight seldom ends with the death of the weaker, which is generally able to break away and escape. Observations on animals in the restricted environment of captivity, where the victor kills the vanquished because it cannot escape, give no reliable conclusions about what happens in the wild.

Overt fighting usually ends with the submission of one of the contestants. The action of fleeing is equally as submissive as the action of the wolf or shrew that throws itself on its back before the victor. Just as the dominant wolf does not go in for the kill when he could so the winning stag, rat, or seal is content with a token pursuit which he quickly abandons to return to his territory or females. Perhaps the pattern of submission in the wolf is correlated with the fact that the wolves of a pack do not hold individual territories so that fleeing would only invite pursuit and could not express submission because there is no territory to vacate in favour of the stronger.

Both overt and ritual fighting show a conflict between the interests of the individual and those of the species. The interest of the individual is to have no rivals for the possession of his territory or females. Carried to its extreme this interest would result in the survival of so few males that the gene pool might become so restricted that the species could not survive. The interest of the species is to keep the gene pool well mixed, and it is therefore probable that natural selection has preserved patterns of behaviour that do not result in widespread slaughter. It may be that species which did not possess such a pattern have by its very absence become extinct.

The suggestion is sometimes made that intraspecific fighting is of survival value to a species because it ensures that the strongest males breed. But there is no proof that these animals will beget better offspring, for it is the genotype not the phenotype that matters— although the strongest phenotype is no doubt the best vehicle for the genotype. In South Georgia during the last forty years the effect of the sealing industry in killing the largest bull elephant seals has been the extinction of the huge "beachmasters" that formerly dominated the harems of cows. The bulls now have a much shorter expectation of life, but were sealing abandoned there is no doubt that in the course of time they would grow into monsters similar to their great grandfathers.

There must be an extremely strong inhibition restraining the victor in a fight from giving the death blow when the rival submits. In man the forebearance might be termed mercy, but ascribing the quality of mercy to animals would be straining things too far. Further work is needed to determine whether the inhibition is innate or learnt, but whatever its origin its effect prevents violent aggressive behaviour within a species from bringing about the death of large numbers of animals. Only one species of mammal habitually disregards it—and he is at present in a very insecure state, in spite of the fact that he is the world's dominant species.

Fatal fighting in man may be associated with the use of tools; it is not easy to kill a rival with the bare hands, though it can be done.

But when tools are used weapons can become so dangerous that a rival can be quickly killed before he has a chance to break away or submit. Man's dentition shows that he is omnivorous—he has always eaten anything good to eat, and often many things that are not. He has, however, been a meat-eater for long enough to have become the specific host of two species of cestode, the tapeworms transmitted by the ox and the pig. When man started using weapons to kill his food it was inevitable that he should use them intra-specifically when family groups came into rivalry. However, in a recent review of Matthiessen's account of the Kurelu people of Dutch New Guinea, Worsley writes: "Yet in spite of the sequence of killing and counter-killing depicted in this book, one has to remember that primitive warfare is distinguished more by sound and fury than by high casualty lists. An isolated killing or wounding is commonly the result of a day's 'campaigning'." In modern life intraspecific fighting is diverted into the variations of the rat-race, and dominance is achieved by success in business, politics, the arts and sciences, although propaganda easily guides the aggressive drive back to its old channels of fighting to kill.

References

Barnett, S. A. 1958. "Social behaviour in wild rats." *Proc. zool. Soc. Lond.*, **130**, 107.
Crowcroft, P. 1957. *The life of the Shrew:* London.
Darling, F. Fraser. 1937. *A herd of Red Deer.* Oxford.
Goodall, J. 1963. "Feeding behaviour of wild chimpanzees." *Symp. zool. Soc. Lond.*, **No. 10**, 39.
Hall, K. R. L. 1963. "Variations in the ecology of the Chacma baboon *Papio ursinus.*" *Symp. zool. Soc. Lond.*, **No. 10**, 1.
Jones, F. Wood. 1924. *The Mammals of South Australia. Part II.* Adelaide.
Lamont, J. 1876. *Yachting in the Arctic Seas.* London.
Pedersen, A. 1962. *Polar Animals* (translated from the French by Gwynne Vevers). London.
Verheyen, R. 1954. *Monographie éthologique de l'hippopotame* (Hippopotamus amphibius *Linné*). Institut des Parcs Nationaux du Congo Belge. Exploration du Parc National Albert. Bruxelles.
Worsley, P. 1963. *Review of Matthiessen, P., Under the Mountain Wall.* London: 1963. Guardian 25. x. 63.

DISCUSSION

HUXLEY: The rare individual male Red Deer with unbranched straight antlers (switches) are reputed to be able to kill rivals relatively easily. There must have been selection against the switch gene, on the basis of its being disadvantageous to the species, though advantageous to its individual possessor. This is a further argument in favour of deer antlers being largely threat-characters, and adapted to avoid killing. Fights between stags are thus essentially ritualized tournaments in Lorenz's phrase.

HARRISON MATTHEWS: Yes, I agree.

STORR: Does Dr. Harrison Matthews consider Man to be a territorial animal?

HARRISON MATTHEWS: Yes, certainly. You have only to notice the sign-boards dotted all over the countryside announcing that "Trespassers will be prosecuted" to realize this. On an international scale what are euphemistically called "deterrents" perform a similar function.

FREEMAN: Is there evidence of an inhibitor mechanism in human beings similar to that found in other animals?

HARRISON MATTHEWS: I have no exact information on this point from primitive cultures, but I have no doubt that there are many greetings and rituals as in modern civilization which has evolved such devices as hand shaking, the offering of cigarettes and similar mechanisms as signs of non-aggression to inhibit attack or at least hostility.

BOURNE: I would like to ask Dr. Harrison Matthews whether he has any evidence of overt killing in the Killer Whale (*Orcinus orca*). I saw members of this species attacking each other off Iceland a few years ago. The Killers had been troublesome to the fishing fleet at the time and depth charges had been used to scare them away; there was no evidence of injury to the animals, but soon after the bombing fighting broke out and continued to break out frequently over the two subsequent days, during which time two animals were seen to be badly damaged and one actually devoured.

HARRISON MATTHEWS: I have not hitherto heard of Killer Whales attacking one another. I think the example quoted can hardly be regarded as normal behaviour if the animals had been bombed with depth charges by fishermen.

RUSSELL: Mr. Fisher has given examples of contemporary clashes between human individuals of different races. He has related these to the aggressive behaviour observed between what were once geographical races of one animal species, when they meet again after the long period of genetic divergence necessary for them to become separate species.

In the first place, in none of these human supposedly racial clashes do we have any means of separating the factors of genetic divergence on the one hand, and generations of divergent upbringing on the other. Merely from these examples, therefore, it is already equally possible that the crucial divergence is cultural and not genetic.

But in the second place, we have abundant examples of aggressive interaction between individuals and societies which are racially homogeneous, where the cultural factor is the only one present. Two examples spring immediately to mind.

The mainland Greeks of classical and Hellenistic times were racially homogeneous. But they split into a number of societies, which showed considerable cultural divergence. Some of these, such as Sparta, were culturally highly specialized. Warfare between the Greek states was endemic for several centuries, and was only brought to an end when the Greeks were conquered by the Romans, who proceeded to enlist them in Roman civil wars.

The region of the Great Wall of China is a striking example. Geographically, this frontier is a band rather than a line, and the Wall was built along several different lines in the course of history. South of the band, there arose a society specialized increasingly for irrigation agriculture. This technique could not be practised far north of the frontier, and the Chinese society excluded the northern peoples from its civilization. The northerners became no less specialized for the quite different technique of pastoral nomadism. The Chinese sought to restrict trade across the frontier, which their own society was too specialized to tolerate. When divergence was nearing completion on both sides, in the Waring States period, work began on the Wall. From then on, warfare between the agriculturalists and the nomads was almost continuous for a couple of millennia, and at times epidemic on a scale rarely paralleled elsewhere. In this instance, only cultural divergence is involved.

An analogy can therefore be drawn between the mutual hostility of animal populations between which the flow of genes is no longer possible, and that of human populations so divergent culturally that communication between them becomes difficult and restricted; though previous absolute geographical isolation seems less necessary in the latter case. Mr. Fisher has therefore drawn attention to a matter of interest and relevance to this symposium. But in human societies, there is every reason to suppose that divergence and breakdown of communication are in terms of culture. It should therefore always be possible to restore communication and peaceful interplay by economic, social and educational means, when we understand enough about human cultural change.

FISHER: I agree with Dr. Russell's last sentence particularly, and with what he says generally. The existence of group aggression *within* a human subspecies and with a cultural basis is undeniable. But to demonstrate it does not even partially negate the existence and also the adaptive significance of taxogenic aggression and other isolative behaviour patterns and drives between what are—or still nearly are—full subspecies of humans, which have become rejungent.

It is true that in parts of the Caribbean and Latin America three such rejungent taxa have widely hybridized and appear to be settling down into a reasonably peaceful phase of genetic reorganization. But two of the same taxa in North America, Caucasoids and Negroids, have gradually come to share much culture, in the sense of household goods and style, and tastes in religion, art and entertainment. Yet the hydridization of the races—although it does not *markedly* occupy a zone as in the classic pattern of racial rejungence—concerns less than ten per cent of each population. The most economic hypothesis is that the situation derives primarily from taxogenic and not from cultural behaviour.

HARRISON: Mr. Fisher has suggested in his paper that aggressive conflict in man is racial in origin and comparable to that found in subspecies or semispecies of birds which are allopatric during development, but later come together and show aggressive behaviour where they meet. In primitive man aggression was surely not a matter of race, but occurred in the first instance between one family and another, or one village and another, where both sides were likely to belong to the same race. This type of aggression would appear to be similar to that shown by birds in normal territorial behaviour between individuals of the same species. Admittedly in man the territory is held by a group and not by one individual but this can be paralleled by some bird species which hold territories which are defended by a group and not an individual. If we look at the history of man there is a considerable amount of evidence to show that areas of land hold a tremendous attraction for men, and that they will defend them and will try to hold on to them even when it has become disadvantageous for them to do so. I think we must consider the possibility that man is, in fact, a territorial individual and not of one species or race against another.

FISHER: Man is indeed a territorial animal. Ornithologists defend their breeding territories and to an extent also their feeding territories in a way closely resembling the objects of their study. Pecking order in institutions closely resembles that of domestic fowl. Group adherence such as that of terns or wild geese is known among humans.

I have been, I reiterate, discussing that kind of racial rejungence after geographical isolation and spread; such as the classic case of the chain of *Larus* gull species that has spread all round the northern world since the end of the last Pleistocene glaciation and has produced five good species from one in a few thousand years. Gull watchers can see taxogenic behaviour for themselves in the rejungent zones of these gull forms, particularly in the Canadian Arctic. On meeting, these had preadaptations not only in structure and particularly recognition colours but also in voice and other behaviour organs.

My thesis is that it is as wrong to deny the existence of certain taxogenic preadaptations and tendencies in human races as it is wrong to believe that human evolution can become truly reticulate without vast self-understanding and education, culminating in self-enforcement.

FREEMAN: Could Mr. Fisher give an example of rejungence of races in the human species?

FISHER: Prehistorically: some evidence of rejungence, that I have already mentioned, between sapient and Neanderthal men, possibly in several places, probably in Palestine. Historically: much in Africa, where the Negroids and their allies were the original race belonging to the Ethiopian fauna, and became rejungent with Caucasoids by the basically Arab invasion from the north and the western European colonization from the south. For taxogenic behaviour, *circumspice*; not only in Africa but—and I quote a fearless, liberal and thoughtful fact-facing analysis in the current *Newsweek* magazine—in North America.

HUXLEY: We must remember that the whites in the U.S. have so little pride in their genetic peculiarities that they officially designate as *negro* any individual with any visible or recorded admixture of negro genes. Thus probably half the "negro" population of the U.S. has a large admixture of "white" genes.

HARRISON: The main point which I tried to make earlier was that aggression in man was basically aggressive behaviour within small similar groups and not between races or cultures. Until recently—certainly until the end of the nineteenth century—a foreigner in an English village might be a man who came from a similar village only a few miles away; and, certainly where children were concerned, such an individual might be the recipient of the redirected aggression of the community.

KALMUS: I think one should point out that the role of aggression in speciation is quite uncertain: while it quite frequently may be a concomitant during the formation of genetically separated groups, there is little doubt that the vast majority of polymorphisms which we must consider to be the incipient phases of species formation have nothing whatever to do with aggression. Neither people nor birds fight each other because of differences in blood antigens or haemoglobin variants, nor have I heard of any aggression caused by differences in PTC tasting. Only those genes which case conspicuous characteristics noticeably for the conspecific aggressor, like peculiar colours, shapes, odours or noises, can become markers and can thus be used as tags in situations of inter-group aggression, arising from quite different causes.

LANE-PETTER: In polygamous colonies or societies there is a surplus of males, and at least in some cases many males will never at any time find a mate. If this surplus was not biologically useful, the evolution of polygamy might have been accompanied by the evolution of an increased sex ratio, or some mechanism for the removal of surplus males, so that the useful members of the species did not have to compete with the celibate males. Yet this does not seem to have taken place. Would Dr. Harrison Matthews like to throw some light on this?

HARRISON MATTHEWS: This is an interesting point on which we should like to have much more information. In some species the subordinate males do not remain celibate, for with patience they may supplant the dominant ones when they are spent towards the end of the rut. In other species they will reach dominance in later seasons; but in many species, such as some seals and primates, there is a great surplus of males which disperse, and what happens to those animals is at present not known.

CULLEN: Dr. Harrison Matthews has contrasted the advantage of ritualized fighting to the species, with its disadvantage to the individual. But it seems very possible that the individual itself also benefits: if it is an animal likely to lose a non-ritualized encounter, it can withdraw without suffering potential injury—so that one can see the value of it responding to ritualized threat. Even for the animal likely to win, there seems a plausible advantage in reducing the chance of injury, however slight, from its rival as well as the reduced alertness to predators which fighting must involve. Should the dominant animal's threat not deter its opponent, it may be followed up, as in many animals, by real attack.

HARRISON MATTHEWS: Yes, it may be followed by real attack but in general such attack only reinforces the threat and the weaker gives way. In either case the biological purpose of the losing individual—namely to reproduce —is frustrated, at least for the time being.

LORENZ: The degree of aggressiveness found in any species is, like that of any other property, the result of several, conflicting selection pressures between whose demands a workable compromise must be effected. It is advantageous for a stickleback to be as aggressive as possible which means the fish must not be so aggressive as to attack his own female. An exaggeration of certain properties is often observed where competition between fellow-members of the species exerts a selection pressure in a certain direction. In this case characters may be evolved which are definitely disadvantageous to the species in its interaction with its extra-specific environment, but indispensable for the propagation of the individual because of intraspecific competition. The antlers of many species of deer are one example of such characters, the secondaries of the Argus Pheasant, *Agusianus argus* L. are another. The bigger these feathers, the greater is the cock's expectation of alluring hens and producing progeny, and, as the power of flight is noticeably reduced, also of being eaten by a predator. Life expectation and attractiveness being in inverse proportion to each other, the actual feather length of the pheasant is a compromise between both selecting factors. As the property produced by intraspecific selection is an "adaptation" to nothing else than another property of the same species, a positive feedback between both can produce a detrimental snowballing effect. Oskar Heinroth used to say in jest that next to the Argus Pheasant's secondary the hustle of western civilized life was the silliest product of intraspecific selection. I think I know a sillier one. When palaeolithic man had mastered his extra-specific environment so far that conflict between hostile neighbouring hordes became the main selecting factor, a tremendous intraspecific selection pressure must have been brought to bear on the development of all "warlike virtues", aggressiveness among them. From the viewpoint of intraspecific selection it is quite easy to understand how many quasi-pathological phenomena have come to pass.

SOLOMON: Ritualized fighting occurs also in some human social groupings. I recall that at my school the boys settled disputes by fighting with their fists: the use of weapons, or even kicking or biting, was not tolerated.

CULLEN: Dr. Harrison Matthews has said that in spite of cropping, the sea-elephants of South Georgia, though not now achieving anything like the size they used to, are nevertheless increasing in number. But this does not show, as he implied, that the animals are today reproductively more prolific than their forefathers, and I should like to ask whether there are direct figures to compare the reproductive potential then and now.

HARRISON MATTHEWS: Dr. Cullen has mistaken my meaning. I did not intend to imply that the animals are reproductively more prolific than formerly. The population has increased because the indiscriminate slaughter of both sexes and the young has stopped and cropping is confined to the bulls, 10 per cent of which are allowed to live. My point was that the genotype is certainly unchanged, although the bulls that now sire the populations are those that formerly would have been subordinate and would have been forced to wait for several years and reach full stature before they could become beach masters and breed.

MORRIS: Dr. Matthews has mentioned the offering of a vulnerable part of the body as an important appeasement gesture. Recent studies have indicated that this particular mode of appeasement is far less common than was once believed. Of greater and more widespread significance are submissive gestures which are the *opposites* of the threat signals of the species concerned. If, for example, an animal puts its head *down* as a threat gesture, then it will put its head *up* as a submissive gesture, or vice versa. Another basic type of appeasement consists of the performance of what I would like to call *re-motivating displays*. These are actions which arouse in the attacker a non-aggressive tendency which then competes with and inhibits the aggressiveness that is present. Two common examples of this, that occur in many species, are pseudo-infantile displays and pseudo-sexual displays. In these instances, the submissive animal performs either juvenile or sexual patterns which arouse parental or sexual responses in the aggressor and in this way stop the attack.

WATSON: Can Dr. Harrison-Matthews give any instances of ritual armament becoming such an embarrassment that it has a deleterious effect upon a species? I was thinking of *Triceratops*, but perhaps his armament might not be considered ritual, and there may be later examples, possibly including man.

HARRISON MATTHEWS: The classical example is the giant Pleistocene deer, *Megaceros*, which is believed to have become extinct at least partly because of the extreme size of the antlers in the males. Even a giant deer must have found it a great strain on its metabolism to grow antlers spanning 10 feet and weighing the best part of a hundredweight and then to throw them away every year. It is probable that an adverse change in the ecological conditions of no great magnitude could be more than it could cope with.

Man has kept his body fairly generalized but has in fact invented armaments as extensions of it. His most popular weapon for self assertion —though not intended to kill—is rapidly becoming an embarrassment as we daily experience in the frustration of traffic jams and chaos in our towns. Many of us now abandon the use of our motor cars in towns and use taxis that we can discard when done with—perhaps we follow in the footsteps of *Megaceros*.

KALMUS: Recently Dr. Butler and his colleagues at Rothamsted found that a newly discovered pheromone caused the unruly and aggressive workers of queenless colonies of honey bees to quieten down. I wonder whether such chemical means are not used in other social insects, in particular in ants, to control aggressive behaviour.

RITUALIZED FIGHTING

By

KONRAD LORENZ

*Max-Planck Institut für Verhaltensphysiologie,
Seewiesen, Germany*

IF WE put together, into the same container, two sticklebacks, lizards, robins, rats, monkeys or boys, who have not had any previous experience of each other, they will fight. If we do the same with two animals of different species, there will be peace—unless, of course, there is a prey-predator relationship between them. Intraspecific aggression, or aggression for short, is found in the vast majority of vertebrates and in many invertebrates. There cannot be any doubt about the important functions it achieves in the interest of the survival of the species.

The first, and probably the most important, of these functions is the spacing out of individuals of one species over the available habitat; in other words the distribution of "territories". Another is the selection of the "better man" by rival fighting, relevant in conjunction with defence of the family or the society by the male;* a third is the establishing of a social rank order which is of particular importance in social animals in which learning is highly developed, so that the individual experience of the aged leader is of great advantage to the community. There are, of course, some other, less important functions of aggression in its simple unmixed form, but they need not concern us here. There are, however, some highly important functions which aggression performs in the system of mutual interactions between independently variable motivations governing animal and human behaviour. Of these we shall talk later.

The selection pressure exerted by all these functions has caused aggression to evolve independently in a great number of different animals, the same performance being achieved by very different means. Very often weapons which originally served functions other than those of intraspecific aggression, were pressed into its service. All these weapons were made to kill, or at least to inflict as serious an injury as possible, as they were primarily adapted to overcome

---

*Without such a correlated other function, rival fighting can lead to intraspecific selection which very often effects evolutionary changes not in the interest of the survival of the species.

a prey or to defend the organism against a predator. In both cases, the damage done to a non-conspecific animal is entirely to the advantage of the species, while the injuries suffered by the combatants in intraspecific fighting clearly are not. Moreover, they are not really necessary for the achievement of any of the functions already mentioned; these are served just as well by a sound thrashing as by a killing. There seem to be very few subhuman species of animals in which intraspecific fights lead regularly to serious wounds and death, which, in these cases, must be regarded as a sacrifice made by the species in order to attain the advantages of aggressive behaviour.

However, very few animals go to these extremes. The only case to my certain knowledge in which the attack of a rival often results in the immediate death of the fellow-member of the species, concerns a lizard, *Lacerta mellisselensis*, in which G. Kramer repeatedly saw one male break another's back by a single bite and twist of the head. In Indian elephants, according to J. H. William's reliable reports, it is also a frequent occurrence that a tusker is mortally wounded in natural rival fighting. Circumstantial evidence makes it probable that mass fighting in rats and other rodents may also lead to the death of individuals under natural conditions. For the rest, I believe that our experience with captive animals and, of course, with our own species, misleads us into overestimating the loss of individuals incurred by intraspecific fighting in most animals.

In the great majority of species measures have been taken to render aggression less dangerous. They may consist of defence movements so well adapted to the species-specific form of attack that the latter is almost invariably parried. (Whoever has witnessed a serious clash between two lions will have been surprised by the total absence of gaping wounds after much roaring, flashing of fangs and pounding of armed paws.) They may also consist of merely passive armour, the fat-padding and the upright mane on the neck of a Przewalsky stallion being good examples. However, in very many cases the necessity of making aggression less dangerous has led to changes in the behaviour patterns of fighting itself, in other words to "ritualization". I cannot go into detailed discussion of the rather complex concept which we associate with this term. Its definition is necessarily an injunctive one, and it is a matter of taste on which of its part-constitutive characters one chooses to put most stress. So I shall not disagree with anyone who contends that the evolutionary changes in fighting, of which I am going to speak now, are not very typical examples of what we call ritualization. However, the ritualized redirected activities of which I am going to talk later on, definitely are.

One line of differentiation which tends to alleviate the damage done to individuals without decreasing the survival value of aggression, is the development of so-called threat behaviour. It invariably arises out of a conflict between the motivations of attack and escape, and in its most primitive forms it may consist of the simple super-position of motor patterns simultaneously activated by both. In many spiny-rayed fish, the aggressive urge to swim at the adversary and the escape drive trying to effect the opposite often results in both combatants turning broadside on at close quarters with heads averted. At the same time aggression induces them to show their most beautiful display colours, and fear causes them to erect their unpaired fins to the utmost. In this broadside-on posturing, there are primarily no appreciable elements of ritualization. But as the attitude automatically displays the full size of the individual to the eyes of the rival, there is obviously a strong selection pressure at work to make the fish appear as large as possible. Unpaired fins have become enlarged, their borderlines enhanced by conspicuous colourations and their erection exaggerated to the point at which the danger of tearing the fin membranes arises. A new motor pattern was "invented", namely the lowering of the radii branchio-stegi in a vertical plane so that the fish's visible contours were enlarged by the spread of the gill membrane; the latter was adorned by new, striking colour patterns. With these additions, all pointing unequivocally to its communicative function, the broadside-on display definitely takes on the character of a ritualized activity.

Even more widely distributed among teleosteans than the broad-side-on display is the tail-beat, very probably a derivative of the former. Standing parallel to the rival with head averted, the fish delivers, in the direction of the adversary, a stiff beat with the maximally spread caudal fin. In some species, in which both fish stand very closely together in display, the rival may be actually swept away by the stream of water thus produced. Even with the mildest forms of tail-beat, the lateral line organs of the reactor must receive a pressure wave indicative of the actor's strength.

Another motor pattern of threat, not quite so widely spread among bony fishes as the two aforementioned, also arose from the conflict between aggression and fear, and also, very probably, evolved independently in several families of fish. It consists in a halfhearted, tentative bite at the other fish's head, very different indeed from the wild ramming thrust launched in uninhibited aggression. The ritualization of this movement is contained more in its releasing mechanism than in its motor co-ordination: it can only be performed if the reactor retaliates in kind. In other words, any intentional movement preparing for this kind of bite is instantly suppressed if the other fish continues to stand in the attitude of broadside-on display. Never, never does a fish bite into the opponent's unprotected flank. As a result, the movement under discussion is fully performed only when both fishes do so simul-taneously, so that they bite at each other's mouth, hence the descriptive term "mouthfighting". From this movement, two lines of differentiation lead up to more ritualized forms. In the genus *Tilapia* both fighters open their mouths as far as possible and push against each other; in *T. mossambiqua* and other species of the genus, the inside of the mouth, particularly the toothed areas, are brightly coloured and displayed a few seconds before the fishes start to push. In other Cichlids, each fish grabs at the other's jaw, takes a firm hold and then pulls for all he is worth. It must be borne in mind that such grasping with the jaws, and particularly pulling at a strongly resisting object, does not occur in any other situation.

All three behaviour patterns just described precede actual fighting. All of them very obviously serve to "size up" the opponent, to measure the fighting potential of one rival against that of the other before damage is inflicted. A small fish may swim up to a bigger one and display broadside-on, but will collapse and flee the moment the other unfolds his unpaired fins and shows his size and colours. If the difference in size and strength between the rivals is slight, matters may proceed to tail-beating and, if still slighter, to mouth-fighting. The combatants must indeed be very equally matched if the observer is to see an actual, damaging fight, which only takes place when the introductory motor patterns have failed to lead to a decision. The damaging fight, in most bony fishes, consists in delivering ramming thrusts at the adversary's flank. As both fishes try to do so simultaneously, this results in their rapid circling round each other, technically termed the "merry-go-round".

In fish, as indeed in most animals, more highly ritualized patterns of fighting have evolved along analogous lines. Almost invariably the threatening behaviour, particularly that part of it, in which physical strength of the fighters is measured *and, at the same time, exhausted*, has developed more and more, *postponing* the breaking-out of damaging motor patterns further and further until, in some species, the latter have become vestigial or have disappeared altogether. In this evolutionary process, changes in the thresholds of the different motor patterns play an important role. We know from the comparative study of closely allied species that quantitative changes in the frequency with which certain homologous motor patterns appear, are the most recent steps in the evolution of behaviour. We know that rareness of occurrence generally means that the motor pattern in question has a higher threshold than other "cheaper" and more frequently shown patterns activated by the same kind of excitation. It is a justified assumption that the differences in the thresholds of the single motor patterns offered a good point of attack to the selection pressure tending to eliminate damage to the individual while preserving the survival functions of fighting.

A beautiful serial stepladder of differentiation can be demonstrated in the fighting behaviour of the many species of Cichlids known to us. It shows very plainly that, in the least differentiated forms, the thresholds of the ramming thrust and the merry-go-round are only very slightly higher than those of broadside-on display and tail-beating. As fighting excitation does not rise smoothly but rather in a saw-toothed curve, the sequence of thresholds leading from display to damaging fight is not directly observable and, in some particularly excitable species, hostilities may even be opened by a ramming thrust that makes some scales fly. In species with a more highly ritualized form of fighting there is a more regular succession of motor patterns showing very clearly their correlation with the several consecutive stages of mounting excitation. With higher ritualization, these stages become progressively more distinct from each other. This has to do with a phenomenon called *typical intensity*, to which Desmond Morris was the first to draw our attention. In most innate motor patterns there is an infinite gradation between slight initial hints of the movement and its full performance. As Erich von Holst has shown, this scale of intensities is very probably caused by slight differences in the thresholds of single neural motor elements: with rising excitation more and more of them are recruited into activity. In some ritualized movements functioning as releasers, the selection pressure exerted by the demand for un-ambiguity of the signal has tended to diminish, if not to abolish, the *variability of form caused by differences of intensity*. Very probably it has done so by pushing up the lowest thresholds and lowering the highest ones, thus narrowing down the intensely-correlated variability of the motor pattern. In some extreme cases, in which all elements concerned burst into activity at the same level of action-specific excitation, the motor pattern actually obeys the all-or-none law quite as strictly as does the function of the single neuron. As a necessary consequence it then appears in one single characteristic and easily recognizable form.

Typical intensity is one of the most important part-constituent properties of ritualized behaviour. Indeed it is the character by which we usually first diagnose ritualization in a hitherto unknown motor pattern. We are so accustomed to meeting intensity-correlated variability in the behaviour of all humans and animals surrounding us, that it at once strikes us as something artificial or ceremonious if we are confronted with typical intensity in any motor patterns. This, indeed, is one of the many amazing analogies existing between phyletic and cultural ritualization. Practically all behaviour rendered *"formal"* by the latter is characterized by being what we call *"measured"*. The measure thereby implied is that of typical intensity. Some of the films which I am going to show will, I hope, demonstrate this point convincingly.

We are better informed about the evolution of ritualized fighting in Cichlids than in any other group of animals I know of. But it is to be inferred that forms of intraspecific aggression which achieve their survival functions without doing damage to individuals, have evolved independently, but along analogous lines, in very many other vertebrates. Among lizards of the genus *Lacerta* there are, as already mentioned, species with the most deadly damaging fighting known among subhuman vertebrates, but there are other species of the same genus in which the whole combat consists of a strictly fair wrestling match. In *Lacerta agilis* the males first stand parallel to each other facing in opposite directions, head to tail, each animal flattening its body by active movements of its ribs in such a manner, that it becomes high and narrow, thus increasing its contours as seen from the rival's viewpoint. The green flank as well as a lateral part of the yellow belly are flattened into a vertical plane, offering a striking colour display. After a short time of this highly ritualized threat, both males tilt their heads slightly towards each other, actually offering the heavily armoured occiput to be bitten. Usually it is the weaker animal that takes hold first and tries to shake the opponent. If the latter is much heavier, it often gives up and goes into a submissive attitude even before getting bitten itself. Otherwise there is a regular alternation of bites, every lizard desisting after a ritually determined time and offering, in turn, its occiput to be grabbed by the opponent. Neither G. Kitzler, who very thoroughly investigated the lizards here mentioned, nor myself ever saw a *Lacerta agilis* bite another in any place other than the occiput, nor did we ever observe any other form of damaging fight. The same is true in *Lacerta strigata major*, in which, most surprisingly, the males grab each other at the proffered knee and, thus linked into a circular arrangement, dance round each other in a wrestling match strongly reminiscent of a certain Swiss national sport, the "Hosenwrangeln".

Some reptiles have developed forms of ritualized fighting in which the mouth and the teeth are not used at all. The males of the Marine Iguana, *Amblyrhynchus cristatus*, push against each other with their heads which are heavily armoured with large protuberant scales; those of many kinds of poisonous snakes of the order Viperidae perform a complicated wrestling match. The selection pressure causing the complete disappearance of biting seems to have been a different one in both of these cases.

I. Eibl-Eibesfeldt is very probably right in supposing that the extremely sharp teeth of *Amblyrhynchus*, adapted to scrape hard growths from submerged rocks, would do too much damage if used in the frequent territorial fighting of males. This is borne out by the fact that the females of the species, indeed more deadly than the males, hurt each other grievously when, after a short introductory bout of head shoving, they proceed to a damaging fight using their teeth. This, however, they do only once a year when contending for nesting sites, and that only in the one subspecies *A.c. venustissima* which lives on an island where egg-laying sites are scarce. Very probably in vipers the story is a different one. Though immune to their own species' poison, these creatures cannot afford to risk their highly vulnerable hunting weapons in rival combat.

All ritualized fighting which has completely done away with damage inflicted on the combatants but which achieves a decision by the mere exhaustion of one of them, can fulfil its essential survival function only on the condition that the vanquished individual is as effectively and as permanently subdued as if it had suffered serious wounds. Although this is a perfectly logical postulate, one is again and again surprised to observe how completely the loser of a ritualized fight is intimidated and how long he retains the memory of the victor's superiority. It is to be supposed that a very special mechanism must be necessary to make the experience of a lost battle so impressive, in spite of the lack of any bodily damage.

I now come to an entirely different type of ritualized aggressive behaviour which, though more specialised and found in much fewer organisms, seems to me to be of greater importance to our understanding of social behaviour in the higher vertebrates and in Man. It is a fact worthy of deep meditation that, for all we know, the bond of personal friendship was evolved by the necessity arising for certain individuals to cease from fighting each other in order to combat more effectively other fellow-members of the species. It is easy to visualize behaviour mechanisms accomplishing a concerted unanimous attack of many individuals on a non-conspecific enemy. Very many animals are known in which a specific "mobbing" signal elicits an intense and universal attack on a potential predator. Such a response can be blindly mechanical and does not necessitate individual recognition between the creatures participating in it. The problem to be solved by evolution becomes much more difficult when the "enemy" to be attacked is himself a fellow-member of the species. The mates of a pair of Cichlids, defending their territory and their brood against hostile neighbours, stand in dire need of all the aggression they can muster, but they must not fight each other, in spite of the fact that each of them, in its striking aggressive colouration and intense threatening behaviour, offers nearly as good stimulation to attack behaviour as does the neighbour that has to be repelled.

Evolution has found a really brilliant solution for this difficult problem. We know from many other observations that aggression, though evoked by one object, can be easily directed towards another, if inhibitory factors prevent its discharge in the direction of the primarily eliciting stimulation. N. Tinbergen has called this process redirection. In the case of our Cichlids, there are two inhibitory factors tending to deflect attack from the mate and redirect it at the territory neighbour. One is sexual motivation counteracting aggression, and the other, much more interesting one, is habituation, one mate getting habituated to the other as an individual. This, of course, presupposes a faculty for personal recognition. I here defy the philosopher to tell me that a fish does not have a "persona": if it has enough personality to be recognized by another fish as an individual, I regard this as sufficient justification for speaking of personal recognition, especially as it is in a very definite "role" —Latin "persona"—in which the partner is recognized.

In most Cichlid fishes, the obviously immense survival value of attacking the territory neighbour in preference to the mate has caused the redirection mechanism accomplishing this to be ritualized into a reliably rigid ceremony. The motor elements involved retain the form of the patterns of threat behaviour already described, except that they are welded into a fixed sequence and invariably directed, as a final goal, against an object other than the mate. One partner approaches the other in the attitude of broadside-on display and may even deliver a tail-beat or two directed at its mate. But while doing so it does not come to a full stop, as it would if threatening an enemy; on the contrary, it lays a visible and very expressive emphasis on the fact that it is moving and keeps moving towards another goal. Immediately after this ceremony, the fish rushes off in the direction of the territory border, quite literally looking for trouble. The reliability of the mechanism deflecting aggression from the mate still hinges, in most of the Cichlid species, on the possibility of discharging an attack against a hostile neighbour.

B. Oehlert, my daughter-in-law, found that she could keep Orange Cichlids, *Etroplus maculatus*, in permanent marital peace only if she kept two pairs, separated by a clear glass pane, in one tank. It sounds like a joke that her attention was regularly drawn to algal growth rendering the pane opaque by the observation of male *Etroplus* beginning to treat their females in an unkind manner. Cleaning of the glass at once re-directed aggressive behaviour towards the neighbour and restored peace between mates. The beautiful energetic economy of the behaviour mechanism under discussion lies in circumventing the necessity to suppress aggression: far from being suppressed, the aggressive drive aroused by the presence of the mate is actually exploited to perform the all-important function of territory defence.

There are, however, more far-reaching consequences to the ritualization of re-directed attack. Whenever ritualization has the effect of welding together, into one obligatory sequence of movements, a number of hitherto independent elements of behaviour, the whole sequence assumes the character of an independent fixed motor pattern with all its physiological properties. It is linked to its own releasing mechanism and, in case the stimulus situation activating it is withheld, it activates its own appetitive behaviour directed at its consummation. Now the releasing mechanisms of all ceremonies derived from redirected aggression contain, as their most important element, an individually acquired familiarity with the area to be defended; so do the mechanisms releasing ritualized redirection of attack depend on the acquired familiarity and acquaintance with an individual fellow-member of the species. In other words, any organism possessing a ceremony derived from redirected aggression is bound to the individual object of this activity with very similar and just as strong bonds as a highly territorial animal is bound to its home. Monika Meyr-Holzapfel, in trying to find an objective expression to describe, in animal sociology, what we would simply call a friend in common parlance, has coined the term "the animal with the home valence". I don't think I could find a more honorific title for my wife.

Indubitably, ritualized aggressive behaviour is at least one root of bond behaviour. The latter can be defined as the keeping together in space of two or more individuals by a set of responses which each of them selectively elicits in the other. We neither know whether all bond behaviour has arisen out of aggression, nor whether ritualized redirection of aggression is its only origin. Both are certainly true for ducks and geese, which have been extensively and intensively studied by ethologists in the last decades. The bond of lifelong individual friendship keeping together wild geese and determining, by its immense strength, the whole structure of their society, is demonstrably based on the so-called triumph ceremony which, also demonstrably, originated in a way strictly analogous to that of the ritualized redirected attack in Cichlids I have tried to describe.

There may be other independent ways in which bond behaviour has evolved, but wherever it did, it seems to have done so as a means of controlling aggression, that is to say on the basis of aggressive behaviour pre-existing. In the Canidae for instance, in the dog-like carnivores, all gestures and ceremonies of greeting, love and friendship are obviously derived from the expression movements denoting infantile submission. It is quite conceivable that appeasement ceremonies, with higher ritualization, have become independently autochthonous motor patterns whose performance constitutes as great a need for the organism as does that of ritualized redirected aggression in the case of the geese's triumph ceremony.

How much of the primarily motivating aggression may still be contained in ritualized redirected attack, or, for that matter, in any behaviour patterns affecting bond behaviour, cannot be deduced from their similarity to or dissimilarity from threat and fighting, but must be investigated separately in every single case. In the triumph ceremony of geese there is certainly quite a lot of autochthonous aggression, as can be demonstrated in the quasi-pathological case of homosexual gander pairs. In these, bond behaviour is much more intense than it ever is in normal heterosexual pairs, occasionally reaching a truly ecstatic climax. As in other known cases, abnormally high intensity of ritualized activity causes true aggression in Freud's sense, that is to say to a recrudesence of the phylogenetically older, unritualized behaviour patterns. In other words, ritualized redirection suddenly breaks down and the partners proceed to fight with a fury never otherwise observed in goose combat. In Cichlids, even under normal circumstances, the danger of redirection failing and attack being launched at the mate, is forever present. In homicide as every policeman knows, the loving spouse is the most likely suspect, the word "loving" emphatically not being used ironically.

The strongest reason, however, which makes me believe that all bond behaviour has evolved, by way of ritualization, on the basis of intraspecific aggression, lies in an unsuspected correlation between both. We do not know, as yet, of a single organism showing bond behaviour while being devoid of aggression; in a way, this is surprising, as, at a superficial appraisal, one would expect bond behaviour to evolve rather in those highly gregarious creatures which, like many fish and birds, live peacefully in large schools or flocks, but this obviously never happens. The great assemblies of these animals are always strictly "anonymous", even in birds of such high organization as starlings, as G. Kramer has conclusively shown. The dependence of bond behaviour in intraspecific aggression is most strikingly demonstrated in those species in which a regular seasonal change takes place between aggressiveness and schooling or flocking. In these cases, whether they concern fish or birds, all individual ties are dissolved immediately when the organism changes from its aggressive to its non-aggressive phase. Also, there seems to be a strong positive correlation between the strength of intraspecific aggression and that of bond behaviour. Among birds, the most aggressive representatives of any group are also the staunchest friends, and the same applies to mammals. No more faithful friendship is known in this class than that which S. Washburn and I. de Vore have shown to exist among wild baboons, while the symbol of all aggression, the wolf, whom Dante calls the "bestia senza pace", has become "man's best friend", and that not on the grounds of properties developed in the course of domestication.

Of course, the relationship between bond and aggression is entirely one-sided. We have reason to believe that intraspecific fighting evolved millions of years earlier than bond behaviour, as indeed all present-day reptiles show the first, while being entirely devoid of the second. But, to the best of our knowledge, bond behaviour does not exist except in aggressive organisms. This certainly will *not* be news to the student of human nature, to the psychiatrist and the psychoanalyst. The wisdom of the old proverbs as well as that of Sigmund Freud has known for a very long time indeed how closely human aggressiveness and human love are bound together.

In conclusion of this highly condensed and correspondingly incomplete presentation of ritualized intraspecific aggression and of its most important consequences, I want to add a few words which, I hope, may stimulate discussion. When Julian Huxley, nearly thirty years ago, coined the word ritualization, he used it, without any quotation marks, for a phylogenetic process as well as for a cultural one; in other words, the conception he associated with the term was purely functional. The functional analogies of phylogenetic and cultural ritualizations are indeed so profound and reach into such amazing details that a conception embracing both is fully justified. Indubitably, one of the most important functions phyletic ritualization has to perform in the interest of a species' survival, is the one discussed in this paper, the controlling of intra-specific aggression. It is to be hoped that cultural ritualization will prove able to do the same with that kind of intraspecific aggression in Man which threatens him with extinction.

There cannot be any doubt, in the opinion of any biologically-minded scientist, that intraspecific aggression is, in Man, just as much of a spontaneous instinctive drive as in most other higher vertebrates. The beginning synthesis between the findings of ethology and psychoanalysis does not leave any doubt either, that what Sigmund Freud has called the "death drive", is nothing else but the miscarrying of this instinct which, in itself, is as indispensable for survival as any other. In this symposium there has been a most satisfying agreement, on this point, between psychiatrists, psycho-analysts and ethologists.

However, it comes very hard to people not versed in biological thought to concede that Man, with a capital M, still does possess instincts in common with animals. That particular kind of pride which proverbially comes before a fall prevents men from under-standing the workings of their own instincts, including that of aggression. As it is causal insight alone which can ever give us the power to influence chains of events and to direct them to our own ends, it is highly dangerous to assume the ostrich attitude in respect to the nature of human instincts. Science is often accused of endangering humanity by endowing it with excessive power over nature. This reproach would be justified only if scientists were guilty of not having included Man among the objects of their research. They have indeed done so, but they have earned no thanks in return. Men like to think of themselves as something outside and above nature. They dislike hearing what a small part of nature they really are and they hate the thought of being subject to its universal laws. They burned Giordano Bruno when he told them that their planet was only one particle of dust in one small dust cloud among innumerable other, bigger ones. When Charles Darwin discovered that they are descended from animals, they would fain have burned him, too, they did their best to silence him in other ways. When Sigmund Freud undertook to investigate the deeper springs motivating human social behaviour, by methods which, though implying the study of subjective phenomena, still were those of inductive natural science, he was accused of lack of reverence, of materialistic blindness to all values and even of porno-graphic tendencies. Humanity defends its self-conceit with all means, fair and foul, and it seems sadly necessary to preach that kind of humility which is the prerequisite for recognizing the natural laws which govern the social behaviour of men.

To put it very crudely: If we know enough about the functions of our intestinal tract to enable medical men to cure many of its disorders, we owe this ability, amongst other things, to the fact that men were never prevented by excessive respect from investigating the physiological causality prevailing in the workings of their bowels. If, on the other hand, humanity is so obviously powerless to stem the pathological disintegration of its social structure and if it behaves, as a whole, in no way more intelligently than any species of animals would under the same circumstances, this alarming state of affairs is largely due to that spiritual pride which prevents men from regarding themselves and their behaviour as parts of nature and as subject to its universal laws.

AGGRESSION IN MONKEY AND APE SOCIETIES

By

K. R. L. HALL

University of Bristol, England

Introduction

THE term "aggression" in its precise sense refers to fighting and means the act of initiating an attack (Scott, 1958). However, as is clear from other contributions to this Symposium, the kinds of behaviour shown by different species of animal in trying to gain ascendancy over conspecifics often fall far short of actual fighting, at least in the natural environment, being expressed in ritualized displays and threat intention movements which are seemingly effective in furthering the survival of the species. In other words, aggressive behaviour is usually, under the ecological conditions of natural feeding, breeding, and defence, adaptive.

In considering the evidence on aggression in the nonhuman primates, no discussion on the Prosimiae will be included, and examples will be taken from those species of monkey and ape on which most systematic field data are now available. Even for these species, however, much remains to be learned about the factors which determine the forms and frequencies of aggression in the natural living groups or populations, the behavioural data being almost entirely at the essentially descriptive stage, with very few studies being taken further, by experiment or controlled observation, to the analysis of causes.

Monkeys and apes, in common with other animals including man, demonstrate aggressiveness by a variety of actions and expressions involving face, limbs, and the whole body. Threat, as the prelude to attack, is expressed in species-characteristic behaviour patterns, including vocalizations, the repertoire of these now being fairly well known for the rhesus macaque (Hinde and Rowell, 1962; Rowell and Hinde, 1962) in a captive group situation, for baboons (Hall, 1962a; Hall and DeVore, in press; De Vore, 1962; Kummer, 1957; Kummer and Kurt, 1963), for patas monkeys (Hall, Boelkins and Goswell, in press), for gorillas (Schaller, 1963), and for chimpanzees (Goodall, in press). Other species that are or have been thoroughly studied in the wild, such as the common langurs, and the vervets, at present lack a detailed inventory of their attack-threat behaviour, and only very recently has an account appeared in English of the communication behaviour of the Japanese macaque (Miyadi, 1963). In terms of thorough ethological description and analysis, all these studies are in some degree deficient, but, for the present purpose of attempting to work out the role of aggression in the natural populations, there is sufficient information for a broad assessment, though not for a detailed quantitative comparison.

Again as in other animals, we find that aggression is expressed not only in direct and seemingly unequivocal forms but in indirect ways where, as is very commonly the case, other motives than to attack are also aroused in the situation, or where direct attack is frustrated. Thus we see from field studies many instances in which a redirection of aggression occurs away from the primary objective or cause of aggressive arousal. For hamadryas baboons, this has been well described by Kummer (1957), and for other baboons by Hall and De Vore (in press). It probably occurs in all species, but the clearest examples, as in the baboon studies, are manifested when a dominant animal is inhibited from attacking another animal of its group of more or less equal status, and diverts its attack onto subordinates. Where, from the context of the behaviour, the motives of attack and escape are simultaneously aroused, both may receive expression in alternating behaviour patterns, or neither may receive expression, only signs of nervousness, such as increased scratching, food-fumbling, and possibly yawning (Hall, 1962b), being in evidence.

Elementary derivatives of threat-intention, or nervousness, or both, have been recorded for several species, as, for example, when branches, twigs, leaves, pebbles, or faeces, are dropped apparently with reference to the position of the human observer (Hall, 1963a). Throwing, or even stick-brandishing, is not uncommon in captive monkeys and apes. Most of these acts seem to have the purpose, where purpose rather than the accidental outcome of agitation can be established, of getting rid of a disturbing stimulus, and not of attacking it. In trying to characterize the nature of aggression in these species, the behavioural "status" of such acts as these is not at issue, although it may later require brief discussion in considering certain implications for human evolution.

No discussion in detail will be included on one limited aspect of aggression, namely the killing of other animals for food. This propensity has been fully authenticated for baboons (Washburn and De Vore, 1961; Dart, 1963), and for chimpanzees (Goodall, in press), the victims being buck of various species, sheep, and, on two occasions, other nonhuman primates (baboon eating a vervet monkey; chimpanzees eating a red colobus). The reasons for omitting further discussion of this interesting habit are, firstly, that far more evidence is required, and could fairly easily be gained, for regional variations in baboons in this respect; secondly that it is not clear at what level of prey we need to look for some evolutionary significance—for example, patas monkeys hunt and eat lizards, vervets eat eggs and fledgeling birds, and so on; thirdly, it is not clear that this propensity has any bearing upon the major aspects of aggression with which we are concerned, namely aggression within and between groups of the same species.

It is similarly very difficult to know how any of these monkeys and apes deal with predators. Goodall (in press) has no evidence that chimpanzees are attacked by leopards. Schaller (1963), though recording that mountain gorillas are occasionally killed by leopards, has no data as to how a gorilla group reacts on detecting their presence. Baboons have been described by Bolwig (1959) as teasing lions. Washburn and De Vore (1963) have a film record of encounters between baboons and lions and cheetahs. Stevenson-Hamilton (1947) observed a large cheetah being chased away by a large male baboon after the former had tried to cut out some juveniles from the group. Loveridge (1923) describes the "mobbing" of a leopard by E. African baboons, "the four old baboons surrounding a leopard and striking at it with their hands" (p. 728). It is also widely known that baboons will turn on dogs that threaten their group. Except for baboons, however, there is so little evidence of defensive aggression in monkeys and apes that we cannot attempt any comparison on this basis as between species. The other large terrestrial monkeys, such as mandrills, drills, and the gelada, have not yet been studied in the wild, and the data on this aspect of aggression in the hamadryas is not yet available from the Kummer and Kurt study. All the evidence suggests that the terrestrial patas monkeys must rely on dispersal and concealment to avoid leopards or hyenas or hunting dogs (Hall, in press), and it is difficult to imagine that this species would do otherwise if encountering cheetahs. Nothing seems to be known about the behaviour of macaque species towards predators.

It is usually supposed that the pronounced sexual dimorphism apparent in baboons (the adult male with well developed canines, being about twice as large and heavy as the adult female) is the consequence of selection pressures derived from their savannah-ranging habits and the need for defence against the large carnivores (De Vore, 1963). Correlated with this is a highly-developed aggressive potential. Equally, if not more, important, however, from the point of view of group survival, would seem to be the very strong social facilitative effect amongst the males consequent upon aggressive arousal by one of their number against a predator-stimulus. All the males are likely to join in the attack if the intensity of arousal is high, but it seems that only the younger, peripheral males may initiate and maintain alarm and defensive behaviour on other occasions, the dominant males remaining in the background. A similar facilitative build-up of attack is reported for chimpanzees in captivity (Yerkes, 1943), and is no doubt well documented for other species.

In patas, likewise, the sexual dimorphism of the adults is very

pronounced, with comparable differences in the canine teeth development, but it seems probable that this functions very differently in
the context of group survival. In each of the groups so far studied,
there has been only a single full-grown male whose conspicuous
size and colouration seemed, from his behaviour, to function in
diverting attention from the group and in enabling the group itself
to maintain contact in the long savannah grass by marking on him
as he sat or stood high up in some tree. It is difficult to imagine,
from the slender physique and the elusive habits of the patas, that
this male alone or the group with him would resort to attacking any
of the large carnivores as a means of defending themselves.

Review of Field Data

The field study evidence will be discussed primarily in terms of
the role of aggression within the group and between groups of the
same species. On the whole, relationships between groups of
different species of monkey or ape are characterized by tolerance or
just ignoring each other. Multi-species aggregations are not
uncommon in certain forested habitats (Haddow, 1952; Reynolds,
1963), and Hall (in press) saw no instances of aggression as between
groups of baboons, patas, and vervet monkeys when these encountered each other in the woodland savannah. It is, of course,
likely that groups which encounter other species groups regularly
in their habitat know very well the tolerance limits to be observed
on such occasions. Between-species chases, or withdrawals by one
species group from the vicinity of another, do occur, but inter-species
group fights have only, it seems, been reported for geladas against
hamadryas baboons in Ethiopia (quoted by Zuckerman, 1932,
p. 195), but such accounts need verification. It is difficult, likewise,
to know how much truth there is in the many stories from different
parts of Africa in which baboons are reported to have attacked
and even killed human beings. Male baboons, in particular, may
become quite fearless if conditioned to expect food from human
beings, and may attack a person in trying to get food (as has occurred
at the Cape, South Africa). No field observer has, however, reported
being attacked by uncontaminated wild groups. On the contrary,
these groups tend, initially, to be very shy, and only gradually, with
habituation, allow of close approach.

(1) Baboons and Macaques

In dealing with all examples from the field literature, aggression
within species groups and between species groups will be treated
as two distinct but closely related aspects of the same social process.
It has generally been considered that the baboon and macaque
genera contain species which are more overtly aggressive in both
within-group and between-group interactions than any other monkey
or ape species. As has been already stated the ground-ranging habits,
taking groups away from refuges of trees or cliffs, are suggested to

have set a premium on the collective aggression of adult males. So far as the genera are concerned, however, it is to be noted that the species of macaques show, from the sampling of rhesus, Japanese, and bonnet, very considerable variations in the extent to which aggression seems to be expressed in the wild groups. Further, from captivity reports, both the stump-tailed macaque, *M. speciosa* (see Kling and Orbach, 1963) and the pig-tailed, *M. nemestrina*, are docile and easy to manage in captivity in comparison with *M. mulatta*.

In the baboon genus, systematic field studies are at present available on *hamadryas* in Ethiopia, on *cynocephalus* in Kenya, and on *ursinus* in Southern Africa. Other large terrestrial species sometimes included in *Papio*, but more usually given separate generic status, are the mandrill, drill, and gelada, on which no field data are available. In reviewing the evidence that is available, one cannot fail to be impressed by the apparent regional variability in aggressiveness shown by *Papio* groups, and it is necessary to be very careful in evaluating these differences in the light of ecological variants that may determine them.

The description concept that most nearly represents aggression in its various forms in these animals is that of dominance. The ordering of relationships within baboon groups of *ursinus* and *cynocephalus*, as outlined by Hall and De Vore (in press), indicates that the large adult males do, on occasions, behave aggressively to other members of their group in a variety of different situations, as where priority of access to a special food incentive or a fully-oestrous female is at issue, or where a female with a young infant has been molested by another female, or where there is a quarrel amongst subordinate members of the group. However, it is obvious from many days of observation of these groups that the routine behaviour of their members is controlled as much by a conditioned expectation of reprisal for what we may call a non-conformist action than by overt threat or attack. When dominance relationships amongst the adult males are clearly established, threat episodes amongst them will be rare, the subordinate simply keeping away from the superior, as in the food-test situation shown in the Washburn and De Vore film. Dominance is manifested aggressively as between the males when tension is aroused by the presence over a period of days of only one female in oestrus, "harassing" threat sequences occurring, as reported by De Vore (see Hall and De Vore, in press). Relative rank amongst the males is also complicated by temporary alliances between, for example, two males who act together in threatening another male who, individually, is described as superior to either of the other two. Fighting amongst the adult males is extremely rare, the demonstrations between them consisting mainly of, to the onlooker, impressive, noisy chases without physical contact being made. These "threat displays" are probably less stereotyped than those described for other nonprimate mammals, but are likely to have the same social significance. Discipline within the group is usually very adequately maintained by threat, or by beating and biting of the subordinate on the nape of the neck which very rarely result in any visible injury to the victim.

The overall picture of group organization in these animals is of a sensitive balancing of forces, the balance being achieved by the social learning of individuals in the group from time of birth to adulthood, so that infringements of the group norm are rare. When they occur, they may be severely punished *if* the victim is caught. Even changes in dominance rank amongst the males are reported to occur as a consequence of persistent harrying rather than by fighting. In other words, physical prowess may not be actually tested, the confident usurping animal achieving his end simply by some of the forms of threat display and moving towards the other animal. What exactly is the social context from which such a usurpment takes place is not yet known. From the Japanese macaque studies, it is likely that the confident attitude of the to-be-dominant male is engendered by his being the offspring of a female who is high in the female hierarchy and hence is closely associated with the already dominant males.

As no full account of the *hamadryas* study is yet available, it is possible only to point out that dominance relations amongst males are quite differently organized in this species. Because the social unit is the one-male party, the male having with him a few adult females and their offspring, dominance is manifested aggressively mainly in the adult male herding his females and preventing any from straying to other units. This exclusiveness is an alternative method of avoiding tension leading to fighting between the males.

Relationships between baboon groups are characterized by mutual tolerance or mutual avoidance according to the nature of the habitat. Where water needs have to be satisfied at a common source, as happens in Southwest Africa, Southern Rhodesia, and Kenya, groups may even intermingle temporarily, then divide up and go their separate ways into their home ranges. Where, as in the Cape of South Africa, or in Murchison Falls Park, Uganda, the need for congregating does not normally arise, groups very rarely meet. Although they overlap into each other's home ranges, and even use the same sleeping cliffs on different nights, they keep apart from one another. No aggressive interactions between groups have ever been recorded by Hall and DeVore (in press) in over 2,000 hours of observation.

What has been said is not intended to imply that baboons are not potentially aggressive to one another. It is all too well known that, in the unnatural restriction of physical and social space of the usual captivity conditions, lethal aggressiveness may occur. As a recent example of this, fighting broke out in a group of 17 baboons at the Bloemfontein Zoo when an "alien" adult male and adult female were introduced into their midst, as a result of which most of the animals were killed or died of their injuries (van Ee, personal communication). The point, of course, is that the natural regulation of numbers within a baboon population, and within the groups that it comprises, is usually achieved entirely by means short of actual fighting. Animals so socially conditionable as baboons have a highly articulated system of appropriate behaviour patterns towards each other, within groups and between groups, so that this tremendous aggressive potential is rarely manifested toward species members.

The social system of the rhesus macaques and the Japanese macaques appears to be similarly constituted. According to Southwick *et al.* (in press), the peculiar habitat of the Temple rhesus groups that they studied led to as much as an 80 or 90 per cent overlap of the home ranges of adjacent groups but these usually avoided contact with each other, as Altmann (1962) observed to be the case with the Cayo Santiago colony, and the "subordinate" group tended to move away as soon as it saw the approach of the more dominant group. Occasionally, however, fairly close contact was not quickly enough avoided, and severe fighting between the two groups would occur. In 85 days of observation, there were 24 severe fights between two of the groups and numerous minor scraps. Normally, the adult males began the fight, but females and juveniles would become involved. Severe wounds often resulted, and most adult males bore wound scars around the face, shoulders or rump. Wounded individuals were fewer amongst rhesus groups in rural habitats and forest areas, where spacing and protective covering greatly reduced the likelihood of intergroup contacts. Baboons have not been studied in a comparable natural situation, but it is reasonable to suppose, by interpolating from captivity situations to the natural ones, that similar manifestations of intergroup aggression would occur.

We have already noted how important a part social facilitation seems to play in the cumulative effect of aggressive encounters. Southwick *et al.* noted that most of the inter-group fights were initiated by young adult (subordinate) males who would normally be the first to contact each other, because of their peripheral position *vis-à-vis* their own group. The sounds of fighting, particularly the vocalizations, would bring more and more animals on to the scene.

From the many years of study of the Japanese macaque groups, group interactions, characterized by tolerance or avoidance, appear to be very similar to those of baboons and of rhesus in habitat areas other than the urban and Temple. Changes in relative dominance as between adult males of a group usually proceed without fighting, and removal of an α male is likely to be followed by a take-over of status by the No. 2 male of the group. The idea that these males, or those in baboon and rhesus groups, achieve their dominance by fighting for it seems mainly to have arisen from inaccurate observations. Threat displays amongst baboon males, for example, may

be exceedingly noisy and vigorous, and give the casual observer
the impression that a kind of dog fight is going on.

For the only other macaque species studied (*M. radiata*, studied
by Simonds, in press), aggression within and between groups appears
to be of much lower intensity and frequency than in rhesus. Males
approach each other for grooming and play, and young adult males
are not forced out to the periphery of the group, as in *fuscata*,
mulatta, and baboon groups. The only threat behaviour recorded
between these groups occurred when a young male dropped out of
a tree into the wrong group, and was chased away. Contacts
between groups were observed on five occasions. When they met,
the young males and the adult males would move towards the other
group, and then sit and look at each other, with distances sometimes
of only about 20 feet separating them. Then the males of one group
would begin to drift back in the opposite direction, and the groups
would separate. No inter-group fighting was observed. Home
range overlaps between groups was of the order of 20 per cent only,
compared with the 80–90 per cent of the Temple rhesus. Probably
this spacing difference is a critical factor. A baboon group in the
Murchison Falls Park was observed to chase another, much larger,
group when the latter had encroached almost to the middle of the
former's home range. This is the only occasion on which a short
chase by a baboon group has been observed. Other contacts between
these two groups, near the respective home range limits, were of
the sort already described as typical of the baboons.

While allowing for the probability that the aggressive potential
may differ in degree from species to species within the macaque
genus, and perhaps also regionally in the baboon genus, such
differences cannot be comparatively assessed without a thorough
knowledge of the ecological circumstances of the group that are
being studied and compared. Under the most widely prevailing
natural conditions, none of these species show aggressive interactions between groups. Where sampling has not yet been very
extensive as in the bonnet macaque study, it remains possible that
other environmental variants may be found to produce a more
aggressively characterized social organisation. In all studies so far
available, however, the effectiveness of the natural controlling
mechanisms are in evidence, so that reduction of numbers through
actual fighting is rarely seen, and the necessary degree of group
cohesion can usually be maintained by occasional threat or by
chastisement short of physical injury. While it seems highly likely
that there are genetic differences in aggressive potential as between
monkey species, the pattern of conformity achieved by members
of a group that live together all their lives is such as normally to
ensure that fighting is extremely rare.

(2) Other Monkeys

Perhaps the most striking comparison with baboons and rhesus
at present available comes from study of the terrestrial patas monkey,

Erythrocebus patas (Hall, in press). Overlapping extensively with baboons and vervets in the Murchison Falls Park woodland-savannah habitat, the species may be expected to have to deal with the same kind of survival problems. Physically, the full-grown patas male is less than half the weight of the full-grown baboon male, but stands almost as high off the ground, and has well-developed canine teeth. These animals are probably the fastest of all primates in running along the ground, being built on the greyhound pattern, rather than for fighting. The adult females are only half the size of the adult males. In each group so far observed, there has been only one large male with several adult females and young animals. Numerical sizes only went up to 23 animals, with an average size for 7 groups of 15 animals. Baboon groups in the same area had a far greater proportion of adult males. In a baboon group totalling 24 animals, there were six large males and nine adult females.

These considerations make it clear that the patas group could not survive predation by leopards or hyenas except by the habits observed in the field, namely dispersion, silence, watchfulness and concealment. Whereas a baboon group tended to cluster together high up in trees by the Nile bank at night, the patas remained out in the savannah, an individual going up into a tree as much as 400 yards distance from the next individual of the group. The group would reassemble about one hour after sunrise, and set off after the adult male on the day range through the long grass and into the erosion valleys. Isolated adult males are occasionally seen near a group or far away from any group.

Within the groups not a single threat-attack by an adult male was observed in over 500 hours of observation. In contrast to the noisy barking and squealing baboons, the patas group is, to the human observer at about 100 yards distance, almost completely silent throughout the day range. As we know from study of a laboratory group of the species (Hall, Boelkins and Goswell, in press), the patas have several distinctive vocalizations in their repertoire, but these are audible only at very short ranges. On not a single occasion, again in striking contrast to baboons, has there been an audible vocalization from the large male or any other animal in the group when the observer has first encountered them or walked too close to them. No animal within these groups had any visible scar or injury. Again in marked contrast to baboons, females or young animals do not show any submissive postures or expressions if the large male passes near to them, nor do they tend to move out of his way. Our laboratory data suggest that adult females may play an important part in regulating the social relationships within the group, and the field data suggest that this large male's main function is watchfulness for predators rather than exerting any aggressive dominance within the group.

On the other hand, the large male patas was immediately aggressive and uttered a higher-pitched baboon-like bark when viewing an isolated male patas or another patas group. No fights were ever seen, nor would ever be likely to occur in such terrain, the isolate or the other group retreating very fast indeed. The patas groups range over a large area of savannah up to about 12 square miles in extent, and, the country being so open, close-range contact between groups is extremely unlikely, especially as the large male tended regularly to go high up into any tree that was available, from which he watched the surrounding countryside.

It would be premature to suggest that this is the "typical" pattern in patas groups, because sampling of other areas, particularly in West Africa, is necessary. Nevertheless, the physical and behavioural adaptations of the patas are clearly understandable in the kind of environment in which they have been observed. In such country, spacing between groups is easily maintained by long-range watchfulness, and there is little or no opportunity for between-group tolerance to be achieved, as in baboons, by a process of habituation. The social order is such as fits the particular environmental needs, and does not require overt aggression to maintain it. Evidently at some stage maturing males must be eliminated from the group, either through aggressive action by the large male, or, conceivably, by concerted action by the adult females. Probably the answer to this important problem can only be provided in the captive group setting.

In keeping with the general picture so far outlined, other monkey species, such as the common langur of India whose physical characteristics and routine behaviour would likewise dispose it to escape or avoid predators, also show far less overt aggression within groups than do baboons and rhesus. "Social relations in a North Indian langur group are not oriented primarily to protection of the individual by group action. Unlike macaques or baboons, a langur protects himself as an individual most effectively by dashing up the nearest tree, instead of depending for protection on large adult males with well-developed fighting powers. Relations among adult male langurs are relaxed. Dominance is relatively unimportant in langur daily life and most of the activities which occupy an individual's time are unrelated to dominance status. Aggressive threats and fights are exceedingly uncommon" (Jay, in press, p. 53). Jay was able to compare langur group behaviour directly with that of rhesus groups in the same area, noting that in the latter aggressive reactions in the group were frequent, and fighting was often severe. In this area, the langurs might spend as much as 80 per cent of the day on the ground, but, as noted, and in contrast to baboons and patas, tended to remain close to trees into which they could easily find refuge. Tolerance between langur groups was likewise the prevailing behaviour.

It will be realized that, so far, only species which spend much of their day time on the ground have been considered, but these samples are sufficient to indicate that it is not terrestrial habit as such which links with aggressive potential but the complex array of physical and behavioural adaptations.

Of the primarily arboreal species, only the South American howlers have been sufficiently studied to afford direct comparison with these Old World species. From Carpenter's (1934) study, it is apparent that dominance relations amongst adult male howlers are far less clearly defined than they are in baboons and rhesus, actual fighting or any form of overt aggression being very rare indeed. Spacing between groups seems to be maintained chiefly by the vocal demonstrations of howler males, and this fits in with the forest habitat which does not allow of visually-derived spacing to be effective. It is an interesting fact that adult male baboons in groups studied in the fairly close woodland areas bordering the Zambesi River (Hall, 1963b) likewise tended to bark persistently in the early morning, these vocalizations being taken up by males of other groups in the vicinity which were completely out of sight of each other. Such vocal demonstrations very rarely occurred in the open terrain of other parts of Southern Africa.

(3) Anthropoid Apes

The study by Schaller (1963) of gorilla groups in a mountain habitat and by Goodall (in press) of a chimpanzee population in a savannah habitat provide important information as to the role of aggression in these primates.

From Goodall's data, it seems that the chimpanzees, in contrast to all the monkey species we have discussed, are loosely organized in temporary parties. Aggressive and submissive interactions between individuals were infrequent, and the concept of a dominance hierarchy amongst the males cannot be substantiated even within the temporary groupings. In the whole of the very long study period, only 72 clear-cut dominance interactions were observed in which one male gave way before another with respect to food or to place. Threat gestures, including vocalizations, were occasionally recorded. Nothing comparable to the between-group tensions sometimes observed in monkeys were recorded, adult males going peacefully from one grouping to another. Even during mating, tolerance between males was in evidence, as when several of them copulated in turn with the same oestrous female. As described by Hall and De Vore (in press), such a situation amongst baboons would almost certainly lead to great tension amongst the males, and, in most groups, the dominant male would have a temporary but exclusive consort relationship with an oestrous female, tending to keep away from the rest of the group, and thus avoiding interference.

The social organization in gorilla groups is similar to that of the monkeys, groups tending to retain their entity. However, although a dominance order is in evidence as between the silver-backed males and younger black-backed males, it is rarely exerted aggressively and interactions between groups were usually entirely peaceable, and sometimes occurred at very close range. The ranging habits of these gorilla groups differed markedly from those of the monkeys, because a group might in successive days, wander over a wide area, its course taking it criss-crossing amongst the paths taken by other groups. Thus, gorilla group home ranges not merely overlap with each other, but seem to be communally shared amongst the gorilla population. No monkey species so far studied has shown a comparable home range pattern, each monkey group, though overlapping with its neighbours, tending to remain most of the time in an area exclusive to its own use.

Conclusion

Although the sample of data we still have available from which to draw comparisons is very limited, and includes only one arboreal species, it is probably sufficient for certain general points to be raised. In common with the comparative treatment of social organization as a whole, it is now obvious that the characteristic expressions and frequencies of aggression within and between groups cannot be meaningfully considered without detailed reference to their ecological context. The large size, the food needs, and the ranging habits of baboons require them frequently to go far away from shelter areas of trees or rocks. Controlled aggressiveness in this context is a valuable survival characteristic in that it ensures protection of the group and group cohesion. Indeed, in a situation where threat to the group arises, the adult males are immediately prominent and the remainder tend to cluster close together. The slim build and speed of the patas who range about as far in a day as a baboon group is correlated with quite a different set of behavioural adaptations, and the physique and habits of langurs and howler likewise are adapted to a relatively unaggressive way of life which is reflected in their social organization. In all the species, however, inter-group spacing is achieved, with the peculiar exception of the Temple rhesus, without fighting, and dominance, in some cases, as between groups ensures the withdrawal of one, just as it ensures the withdrawal of the subordinate individual.

The apes are difficult to place in comparison with the monkeys. Their physical adaptations of great size and strength are far superior to any monkey's, but they are in many respects perhaps less adaptable to survival in the contemporary environment. The relative placidity of the gorilla, coupled with great bulk, slow movement, and apparently restricted diet, put it at considerable disadvantage with the baboons or indeed with the rhesus, patas, or langur. The chimpanzee, with its high rating on the human comparative scale of intelligence, is apparently able to use tools for food-getting and even for defence, and yet lacks other characteristics of social organization and adaptability which must rate it as less successful than the baboons.

The question, of course, arises as to what our knowledge of the different forms that aggression takes in these wild primates has to tell us about the evolutionary role of aggression in the prehominids or early hominids. The closest parallel seems to be discernible in the baboons whose social organization is such as to allow of large groups (up to 200) maintaining their coherence without the aggressiveness of the adult males being in any way dangerous to the survival of the group. The same is true of the relationships between baboon groups, and it is, indeed, a remarkable fact that aggressive interactions between them are so rare, even when ecological needs require frequent and close contact. Probably the most important point to emphasize is that the inhibitory control system of baboon social organization is so effective that their lethal fighting potential is rarely released. One of the most significant tasks for future research will be to work out, under experimental conditions in captive groups, exactly what are the factors of spacing and social learning which determine the natural equilibrium. This equilibrium can, as is already known, be very easily disturbed, and it is necessary that group experiments be conducted to elucidate the tolerance limits in these animals and in other species. If the accounts cited by Dart (1963) and Oakley (1951) for the predatory behaviour of baboons in South Africa can be systematically reinforced in long-term field studies, we have one more line of evidence to support the view, long ago put forward by Carveth Read (1917), that the prehominids may have had many of the characteristics of a wolf-like primate, the nearest contemporary parallel to which is the baboon. The chimpanzee, whom one might assess as academically superior to the baboon, seems to lack other adaptations of a physical and social kind which have resulted in its being biologically less successful.

References

Altmann, S. A. 1962. "A Field Study of the Sociobiology of Rhesus Monkeys, *Macaca mulatta*." *Ann. N.Y. Acad. Sci.*, **102**, 296-315.
Bolwig, N. 1959. "A Study of the Behaviour of the Chacma Baboon, *Papio ursinus*." *Behaviour*, **14**, 136-163.
Carpenter, C. R. 1934. "A Field Study of the Behaviour and Social Relations of Howling Monkeys." *Comp. Psychol. Monogr.*, **10**, No. 2, Serial No. 48.
Dart, R. A. 1963. "Carnivorous Propensity of Baboons." *Symp. Zool. Soc. London*, No. 10, 49-56.
DeVore, I. 1962. "The Social Behaviour and Organization of Baboon Troops." Ph.D. thesis, University of Chicago.
DeVore, I. 1963. "Comparative Ecology and Behaviour of Monkeys and Apes." In: *Classification and Human Evolution*, ed. S. L. Washburn. New York: Viking Fund Publications.
Goodall, J. M. In press. *Chimpanzees in the Gombe Stream Reserve.*
Haddow, A. J. 1952. "Field and Laboratory Studies on an African Monkey, *Cercopithecus ascanius*." Schmidti. *Proc. Zool. Soc., London*, **122**, 297-394.
Hall, K. R. L. 1962a. "Sexual, Derived Social, and Agonistic Behaviour Patterns in the Wild Chacma Baboon, *Papio ursinus*." *Proc. Zool. Soc., London*, **139**, 284-327.
Hall, K. R. L. 1962b. "Behaviour of Monkeys Towards Mirror-images." *Nature, London*, **196**, 1258-1261.

Hall, K. R. L. 1963a. "Tool-using Performances as Indicators of Behavioural Adaptability." *Curr. Anthrop.*, **4**, 479-494.

Hall, K. R. L. 1963b. "Variations in the Ecology of the Chacma Baboon, *Papio ursinus.*" *Symp. Zool. Soc., London*, No. 10, 1-28.

Hall, K. R. L. In press. *Ecology and Behaviour of Baboons, Patas and Vervet Monkeys.*

Hall, K. R. L. In press. *Ecology and Behaviour of Patas Monkeys, Erythocebus patas, in Uganda.*

Hall, K. R. L., and DeVore, I. In press. *Baboon Social Behaviour.*

Hall, K. R. L., Boelkins, C., and Goswell, M. J. In press. *Behaviour of the Patas Monkey, Erythrocebus patas.*

Hinde, R. A., and Rowell, T. E. 1962. "Communication by Postures and Facial Expressions in the Rhesus Monkey (*Macaca mulatta.)*" *Proc. Zool. Soc., London*, **138**, 1-21.

Miyadi, D. 1963. "Studies on the Social Life of Japanese Monkeys." *Proc. Amer. Assoc. Advance Sci.*, December 27.

Jay, P. In press. *The Common Langur Monkey of North India.*

Kling, A., and Orbach, J. 1963. "The Stump-tailed Macaque: a Promising Laboratory Primate." *Science*, **139**, 45-46.

Kummer, H. 1957. "Soziales Verhalten Einer Mantelpavian Gruppe." *Schweiz. Zeitschr. Psychol.*, No. 33, 91 pp.

Kummer, H., and Kurt, F. 1963. "Social Units of a Free-living Population of Hamadryas Baboons." *Folia Primat.*, **1**, 4-19.

Loveridge, A. 1923. "Notes on East African Mammals." *Proc. Zool. Soc., London.* **1923**, 685-739.

Oakley, K. P. 1951. "A Definition of Man." *Science News* (Penguin Books), **20**, 69-81.

Read, C. 1917. "On the Differentiation of the Human from the Anthropoid Mind." *Brit. J. Psychol.*, **8**, 395-422.

Reynolds, V. 1963. "An Outline of the Behaviour and Social Organization of Forest-living Chimpanzees." *Folio Primat.*, **1**, 95-102.

Rowell, T. E., and Hinde, R. A. 1962. "Vocal Communication by the Rhesus Monkey (*Macaca mulatta*)." *Proc. Zool. Soc., London*, **138**, 279-294.

Schaller, G. B. 1963. *The Mountain Gorilla.* Chicago: University of Chicago Press.

Scott, J. P. 1958. *Aggression.* Chicago: University of Chicago Press.

Simonds, P. E. In press. *The Bonnet acaque in North India.*

Southwick, C. H., Beg, M. A., and Siddiqi, M. R. In press. *The Ecology and Social Behaviour of Rhesus Monkeys in Northern India.*

Stevenson-Hamilton, J. 1947. *Wild Life in South Africa.* London: Cassell.

Washburn, S. L., and DeVore, I. 1961. "Social Behaviour of Baboons and Early Man." In: *Social Life of Early Man*, ed. S. L. Washburn. New York: Viking Fund Publications.

Washburn, S. L., and DeVore, I. 1962. Film entitled "Baboon Behaviour." University of California, Berkeley.

Yerkes, R. M. 1943. *Chimpanzees: A Laboratory Colony.* New Haven: Yale University Press.

Zuckerman, S. 1932. *The Social Life of Monkeys and Apes.* London: Kegan Paul.

PHYSIOLOGICAL BACKGROUND TO AGGRESSION

By

Arnold Klopper

*Obstetric Medicine Research Unit (M.R.C.),
University of Aberdeen, Scotland*

IN order to keep the review of this section of the natural history of aggression within a manageable length it is intended to consider mainly the endocrine mechanisms concerned with the physiological background to aggression and to examine the data pertaining to man, making reference to experimental work on other animals only in so far as this reflects on the human situation. It is no accident that the major works in this field, W. B. Cannon's book "Bodily Changes in Pain, Hunger, Fear and Rage" and Hans Selye's writings on stress should both be largely concerned with adrenal function. Most of the endocrine reactions concerned with aggression are mediated through this gland and much the largest volume of endocrine data on aggression pertains to adrenal activity. Much of this review will therefore be concerned with the role of the adrenal in aggression.

In the context of endocrine reactions it is very difficult to find a satisfactory definition of aggression. On the one hand aggression overlaps the emotional states associated with fear, stress and anxiety and on the other hand it cannot be disentangled from the aggressive elements in sexual behaviour patterns. A close definition of the term is not essential to the present purpose and will not be attempted but, where it is known, the point in this emotional spectrum to which a particular experiment refers, will be stipulated.

The Role of the Adrenal in Aggression

In considering the adrenal one is dealing with two physiologically separate glands—the adrenal cortex and the adrenal medulla. Their anatomical juxtaposition is probably not without significance and it will be necessary at a later stage to examine cortical and medullary inter-relationships. In the case of the medulla at least two and possibly three hormones are concerned; adrenaline, noradrenaline and dopamine. The cortex produces a bewildering variety of hormones. For the purpose of discussing the role of adrenocortical hormones in aggression these will be divided into sodium-retaining steroids, exemplified by aldosterone and glucocorticoids affecting carbohydrate metabolism such as cortisol or cortisone. Included in the latter group are steroids having a predominantly anti-inflammatory action.

The Adrenal Medulla

A matter of interest in considering the role played by the adrenal medulla in aggression is the question of how far the hormones cause the emotional state and how far they are the effect or mechanism for conditions arising within the central nervous system. It is difficult to distinguish between the effects of noradrenaline and of adrenaline on the central nervous system but much of the experimental data accumulated in recent years support the view that these two catecholamines can affect the brain tissue directly. Of course they affect the synapses of peripheral nerves directly and in the intact animal it is often very difficult to decide whether a particular effect arises centrally or peripherally. One school of thought holds that all the apparent effects of adrenaline and noradrenaline directly on brain tissue are in fact only an expression of their admitted effect on cerebral blood flow. One central effect certainly is of peripheral origin. This is the inhibition of the vasomotor centre with subsequent bradycardia which is caused by noradrenaline. It is now well documented that this effect is due to impulses from the 9th and 10th cranial nerves from baroreceptor organs in the carotid sinus.

A great variety of effects can be elicited by applying one or other catecholamine directly to cerebral tissue or introducing them into the cerebral arteries. Among the many which have been documented are stimulation of the EEG, wakefulness, lowering the electrical threshold of the motor cortex or triggering of ovulation, all of which appear to be stimulatory responses. On the other hand a series of inhibitory responses can also be set in train, e.g. inhibition of ADH release, suppression of central thyrotropic control, diminution of cortical evoked potentials and the production of stupor. It seems unlikely that all these effects can be accounted for simply on the basis of a general increase or decrease in cerebral blood flow, although the effect of local alterations is not so easy to dismiss.

Any attempt to ascribe a direct central nervous role to the hormones of the adrenal medulla comes against the difficulty that it has been clearly demonstrated that these substances do not diffuse to any extent from the blood into the brain substance. But the brain possesses mechanisms for measuring other characteristics of the blood passing through it—e.g. osmolarity, pH and CO_2 tension and probably the concentration of glucose and steroid hormones as well. It is quite conceivable that there may be detector mechanisms for adrenaline and noradrenaline as well. Marazzi (1958) has put forward the idea that adrenaline has a general inhibitory effect on the synapses of the brain. In those instances where it appears to cause stimulation this is due to the inhibition of inhibitory systems. Other experimental work does not support the view of a general synaptic inhibition. For instance, in isolated midbrain slabs adrenaline increases the firing rate in some cells, decreases it in others, and leaves some unaffected. Vogt (1954) has shown that the highest concentrations of noradrenaline and adrenaline in the central nervous system occur in the reticular activating system. Electrical stimulation of this system duplicates many of the known physiological effects of moderate doses of noradrenaline and of adrenaline. If it is supposed that these catecholamines act at the synapses of the reticular activating system it would explain why potent stimulating drugs such as ephedrine, amphetamine and cocaine should be adrenergic or why tranquillisers such as chlor-promazine are adrenolytic.

As far as aggressive impulses arising from subcortical levels are concerned the hypothalamus seem the most likely source. Roth-baller (1956) has brought evidence to suggest that there are central adrenoceptive mechanisms in the hypothalamus. In his view these receptors are more sensitive to adrenaline than to noradrenaline and it is the former rather than the latter which would be concerned in affective states such as aggression. The hypothalamus contains relatively high concentrations of both noradrenaline and adrenaline and in a few experimental situations what appear to be direct effects of the neurohumours on the hypothalamus can be demonstrated. Thus adrenaline causes marked changes in the electro-hypothalamo-gram and intrathecal adrenaline administration results in hyper-glycaemia. The latter effect is particularly interesting as there is good reason to suppose that the intrathecal catecholamine does not escape into the general blood circulation. It seems more likely that the effect is directly on the cells of the hypothalamus, producing the same result as would an intravascular injection of adrenaline.

There is some evidence to suggest that different catecholamines are associated with different emotional states. From a study of psychotic and psychoneurotic patients Funkenstein, Greenblatt and Solomon (1952) concluded that anxiety is accompanied by increased noradrenaline production whereas aggressive states are character-ized by adrenaline. The role of dopamine in the physiology of aggression is largely a matter of speculation although some inter-esting findings have been recorded. Carlsson (1959) notes that in the mammalian brain noradrenaline and dopamine are present in roughly equal quantities but their distribution is markedly different; dopamine occurs mainly in the corpus striatum and noradrenaline in the brain stem, notably the hypothalamus. Experiments in rabbits suggest that reserpine exerts its tranquillising action by causing the disappearance of noradrenaline and dopamine from the brain tissue.

Carlsson argues that dopamine is involved in the control of motor functions.

Many ingenious experiments have been devised to determine which catecholamine is associated with which emotional state. Elmadjian (1959) compared the adrenaline and noradrenaline excretion of ice hockey players engaged in aggressive skirmishes with that of the goalkeeper waiting anxiously in the rear. He found that active aggressive emotional displays are related to increased excretion of noradrenaline while the more passive anxious role of the goalkeeper was associated with increased adrenaline output. Similarly boxers produced more adrenaline in the tense waiting period before the fight, and more noradrenaline immediately afterwards. Von Euler (1956) assayed the noradrenaline concentration of the adrenals in a number of species and found that aggressive animals, especially felines, have a higher noradrenaline content than non-aggressive species such as the rabbit.

When the effect of aggression on catecholamines rather than of catecholamines on aggression is considered the experimental observations are more conclusive. Forty years ago Cannon showed that the adrenal vein blood of excited animals contained much more adrenergic activity than quiet animals. He used the device of having a dog bark at a cat for half an hour before taking blood from the thoroughly roused feline. Cannon's views have been amply sustained by the development of specific assay techniques for various catecholamines. Modern work has emphasized the importance of psychological as opposed to physical stimuli in causing increased adrenal activity. Thus surgical stress or muscular activity do not cause a notable increase in catecholamine output unless accompanied by pain, fear or anger. Adrenal response does not appear to be specific to a particular emotion but anxiety and anger are the most potent stimuli. The evidence that particular patterns of catecholamine production are associated with certain responses has already been mentioned. It is not possible at this time to put a great deal of weight on the apparent association of noradrenaline with aggression. As far as the physiological effects of noradrenaline on heart and circulation, on smooth muscle and metabolic functions, such as blood glucose levels, or oxygen consumption, can be differentiated from those of adrenaline, there is no reason to suppose that noradrenaline is more suited to enabling an animal to fight than is adrenaline.

The Adrenal Cortex

Two groups of cortical hormones typified by corticosterone and by cortisone are probably involved in the physiology of aggression. The demonstration of a humoral link between the hypothalamus and the adrenal cortex has stimulated interest in the relationship between emotional states like aggression and adrenocortical function. As in the case of the hormones of the medulla some attention has been paid to the role of cortical hormones in causing emotional changes as well as to the effect of such changes upon cortical hormone secretion. Thus it was noticed that patients being treated with cortisone or ACTH for rheumatoid arthritis showed euphoric mood changes which could not be accounted for only in terms of relief of pain. Some subjects may progress beyond euphoria and develop a true psychosis and it was noted that ACTH or cortisone could give rise to mental changes in previously normal people. These findings were reviewed by Allen (1952) who put forward evidence that psychoses are often associated with diseases of the adrenal glands and that in adrenogenital virilism they are sometimes curable by adrenalectomy. It is not possible to show a connection between adrenocortical hormones and aggressive behaviour patterns alone although in general the psychological changes associated with these hormones are of outgoing aggressive nature. Beach (1952) has pointed out that it is unlikely that any type of behaviour is affected solely by one hormone and that it is equally improbable that a given hormone has one and only one effect upon behaviour. In his view adrenocortical hormones exert their effect by altering the functional activities of neural factors controlling the behavioural response. Indeed the psychological response to adrenocortical hormones is largely conditioned by the personality of the recipient, some people becoming alert and euphoric, others restless and irritable.

The power of psychological influences to cause changes of adrenocortical function was noticed almost as soon as means were devised for chemical assay of the steroid metabolites. Rizzo et al. (1954), in studies on a mentally disturbed patient, were able to show a close correlation existed between alterations in his mental state and changes in glucocorticoid excretion. Elmadjian (1955) has published an account of investigations of urinary steroid excretion and protein catabolism in soldiers in various battle situations in the Korean war. He concluded that each of the groups studied—the controls, those in acute combat situations, chronic combat situations, and those who became psychiatrically disturbed showed a different "biochemical profile".

One of the most important developments in the study of adrenal physiology has been the steady growth in recent years of the idea that emotional factors probably play the major part in causing fluctuations of adrenocortical secretion rate in man, monkeys and possibly other species. It is possible that agents such as bacterial pyrogens, histamine or certain peptones can cause a release of ACTH, but neither these nor physical stresses such as pain or cold, are nearly as potent as strong emotion in causing maximal increases in blood cortisol concentration. Thus emotional stimuli such as oral examinations or an interview give rise to blood cortisone levels otherwise only seen in severe Cushing's syndrome.

Some work has been done to determine how far the responses of adrenal cortex and medulla to psychological stimuli are correlated. In many respects these two groups of hormones exert the same effects although by different means. Thus they both counteract hypoglycaemia and protect from damage by histamine. In the terms which Cannon introduced they are both concerned with fitting the animal for fight or flight. In a few particular situations these hormones can be shown to potentiate one another. In acute aggression the output of cortical hormones rises. This is almost certainly the consequence of the release of ACTH from the pituitary which is often accompanied by, and may be caused by, increased medullary activity (Vogt, 1944). The relationship between say, adrenaline and cortisol is not one of simple cause and effect. Although the injection of adrenaline into rats causes a rise in circulating ACTH (Farrell *et al.*, 1952), in man adrenaline does not affect the blood levels of 17-hydroxycorticoids (Tyler *et al.*, 1955). Ramey and Goldstein (1957) summarized the relationships by pointing out that the corticosteroids and adrenalines appear to function as one physiological unit; their sites of action and the tissue and organ responses to them are strikingly similar.

The Role of the Gonads in Aggression

The part played in aggression by sex steroids, testosterone, oestrogens and progesterone is difficult to define. There is a wealth of literature on their relation to sexual behaviour patterns. In such behaviour there are aggressive elements but there is very little data on the relation of sex steroids to purely aggressive behaviour patterns without sexual connotations. Even in very carefully defined and rigorously standardized experimental situations the emotional response to steroids is very variable especially in man and the primates. In part this is because previous conditioning determines behavioural responses to testosterone and oestrogens. Thus a behavioural pattern is "imprinted" with experience, especially sexual experience, which determines the subsequent response to steroids.

The effect of gonadal hormones on aggression becomes more clear-cut in lower animal orders. Thus Guhl (1958) in his studies on the development of social organization in the domestic chick was able to differentiate partly between aggression and purely sexual behaviour patterns. Both male and female chicks treated with gonadal hormones formed peck-rights and a peck-order somewhat earlier than did untreated chicks of the same hatch. Androgenic treatment caused an increase in aggressiveness whereas oestrogen-treated chicks were more submissive.

The influence of sex hormones on behaviour patterns depends not only on previous conditioning, on the particular hormone, the age of the animal, its order and species but even apparently on its sex. Thus throughout the animal kingdom female sexual behaviour pattern is increasingly controlled at a subcortical level as one goes down the evolutionary scale. Females tend, therefore, to be more responsive to sex hormones while, in males of the same species, responses are more modified by cortical influences. There is evidence that sex hormones can influence higher cerebral functions such as learning (Zuckerman, 1952).

Harris (1960) has located two centres in the hypothalamus at which oestrogens act to stimulate or inhibit the release of gonadotrophins. Presumably sex steroids act also at a higher level by influencing the neural mechanisms controlling behaviour, but there is as yet no information where and how they act on the higher centres.

The Role of the Thyroid in Aggression

Many experiments in recent years have shown effects of adrenal and gonadal function on thyroid activity and vice versa. It is to be expected therefore that emotional states such as aggression will have thyroidal effects, if only by virtue of its relationship with the steroid producing glands. It is generally accepted that there is also a direct relationship between emotional states and thyroid function. It can be commonly observed that the thyrotoxic patient is in a state of agitation while the myxoedematous patient is torpid, without overt emotional response. It is widely accepted that emotional factors often play a part in the pathogenesis of thyrotoxicosis and in laboratory animals it is possible to produce marked changes in thyroid function by emotional stimuli such as forced immobilization. Although there is plenty of evidence to connect thyroid function with general stress stimuli there is no reason to conclude that aggressive behaviour patterns have a specific effect on thyroid function or that thyroid hormones condition aggressive behaviour patterns in particular.

References

Allen, C. 1952. *Ciba Colloquia on Endocrinology*, **III**, 180. J. & A. Churchill, London.
Beach, F. 1952. *Ciba Colloquia on Endocrinology*, **III**, 209. J. & A. Churchill, London.
Cannon, W. B. 1920. *Bodily Changes in Pain, Hunger, Fear and Rage*. D. Appleton and Co., New York.
Carlsson, A. 1959. *Symposium on Catecholamines*. Williams & Wilkins Co., Baltimore.
Elmadjian, F. 1955. *Ciba Colloquia on Endocrinology*, **VIII**, 627. J. & A. Churchill, London.
Elmadjian, F. 1959 *Symposium on Catecholamines*. Williams & Wilkins Co., Baltimore. p. 409.
Farrell, G. L., and McCann, S. M. 1952. *Endocrinology*, **50**, 274.
Funkenstein, D. H., Greenblatt, M., and Solomon, H. C. 1952. *Amer. J. Psychiat.*, **108**, 652.
Guhl, A. M. 1958. *Animal Behaviour*, 6, 92.
Harris, G. W. 1960. *Acta endocr. (Kbh)*, **34**, Suppl. 50.
Marazzi, A. S. 1958. *J. clin. Psychopath.*, **19**, 45.

Porter, R. W. 1952. *Amer. J. Physiol.*, **169**, 629.
Ramey, E. R., and Goldstein, M. S. 1957. *Physiol. Rev.*, **37**, 155.
Rizzo, N. D., Fox, H. M., Laidlaw, J. C., and Thorn, G. W. 1954. *Ann. intern. med.*, **41**, 798.
Rothballer, A. B. 1956. *Electroenceph. clin. Neurophysiol.*, **8**, 603.
Tyler, F. H., Migeon, C., and Castle, H. 1955. *Ciba Colloquia on Endocrinology*, **VIII**, 254. J. & A. Churchill, London.
Vogt, M. 1944. *J. Physiol.*, **103**, 317.
Vogt, M. 1954. *J. Physiol.*, **123**, 451.
Zuckerman, S. 1952. *Ciba Colloquia on Endocrinology*, **III**, 34. J. & A. Churchill, London.

HUXLEY: It is clear from the work of Lorenz that ritualization of behaviour serving as a releaser is almost universal in higher vertebrates: (a) so as to make the action more clearly recognizable as a specific sign-stimulus (b) as a method of reconciling conflicts. Lorenz has also always stressed the importance of taking the subjective (emotional) state of the animal into consideration when evaluating its behaviour; this I regard as very important. In this, he is following some of McDougall's ideas. I agree with him as to the importance of McDougall's approach in this respect (though no biologists can follow him in his Lamarckian interpretations).

SOLOMON: Referring to the pair of fishes in which, Dr. Lorenz told us, marital harmony was enhanced by "threat from without"—a pair of neighbours separated from them by a pane of glass converting the tank into semi-detached apartments; would a mirror have been equally effective?

LORENZ: I would not say that "harmony was enhanced" by a threat from without, but the presence of an outlet for aggression is just necessary to prevent intra-marital fighting.

STORR: Professor Eckhard Hess refers in one passage to work done on Cichlid fish in which it was shown that in the male, sexual and aggressive drives reinforced each other but fear inhibited sex; whereas in the female, fear and sex were compatible, whereas aggression inhibited sex. Could Dr. Lorenz comment on this work and say if it is valid, as this finding seems directly transferable to human behaviour?

LORENZ: The work of which my friend Eckhard Hess evidently told Dr. Storr is my daughter-in-law's, then Beatrice Oehlert's. She found that in Cichlids with little sexual dimorphism the only mechanism ensuring heterosexual pair formation is based on a sexual difference in the "mixability" of sexual, aggressive and escape motivation. When two individuals of such a species meet, all three drives are simultaneously activated. Any mixture and superposition of aggressive and escape motivation are possible in both sexes. All "threat" is indeed conflict behaviour motivated by those two drives. In respect to the conflict or superposition of aggression and sex, as well as in that of escape and sex, there is a marked sexual dimorphism. The male is perfectly able to mix and superimpose aggressive and sexual behaviour. He can actually bite and hurt the female, simultaneously performing courtship activities. What he cannot do, is performing such sexual activities while he is afraid of his partner. When escape motivation is ever so little activated, his sexual motivation is down and out. In the female, conversely, aggression does not go with sexual excitation. If the male is too weak to intimidate her sufficiently to exclude all aggressive behaviour, she is nothing but aggressive against him and does not show the slightest hint of sexually motivated activities. Indeed, she is all the more a furious virago, the riper her ovaries and the greater her need for spawning. Fear, on the other hand, does not suppress her sexual drive, quite on the contrary. She can flee and dodge the aggressive male and, simultaneously, perform courtship activities. Ritualization of this type of conflict behaviour is well known as so-called coyness behaviour in many animals. The same mechanism plays an important role in birds with small sexual dimorphism as well, and in answer to Dr. Storr's question whether it also does in humans, I should say yes, indeed, it does.

BROADHURST: In connection with the topic of aggression in primate groups, so ably reviewed by Professor Hall, I should like to make a preliminary reference to some work I have been concerned with but which is being carried out by Dr. S. D. Singh of Punjab University at Chandigarh in India, and which was supported by a grant from the U.S. National Institute of Mental Health (No. M-5263).

We were interested in the effects of urban living in proximity with man on several aspects of the social behaviour of wild rhesus monkeys. India is a most suitable place for such a study since the rhesus monkeys which infest cities in Northern India are under some degree of religious protection there. This species is also to be found in wild groups living in isolation in dense forest. Thus, we have a free-ranging primate which differs substantially in the degree of contact with man. Four different groups were studied, firstly, there were the urban bazaar monkeys, next the temple monkeys, thirdly, those found at canal and roadsides and, finally, the forest monkeys. In this way we tried to sample the range from the most to the least urban. In addition to data on group structure, sexual and grooming behaviour and play, Singh studied aggressive behaviour.

It was found that the incidence of aggression varied with the habitat in the following way. There was significantly more overt aggression in the forest group than in any other, though this aggression was confined to the feeding situation, and occurred principally between adults. Away from the food, on the other hand, there was significantly less aggression among the forest groups, with a steady progression towards a higher level with increasing degree of urbanization. This finding was supported by observations of the greater incidence of severe skin lesions among bazaar and temple groups. Singh explains the lowered incidence of aggression among these latter groups when feeding as being due to the greater frequency of opportunities for sharing food which occur in the urban setting and which gives rise to the development of a tolerance to the frustrations in food getting occasioned both by other monkeys and by humans. It may be that the altered behaviour we are witnessing in these urban groups is a result of the social stresses imposed by the proximity of man, and is partly due to a breakdown of the pattern of dominance obtaining in forest groups which normally gives rise to less overt aggression generally, except at feeding times when the dominance relationships need especially to be reasserted.

These observations require, of course, to be confirmed and extended, but perhaps constitute a beginning to the sort of work which Professor Hall would like to see carried out on induced changes in natural populations.

TARRY: With reference to various points made by Professor Hall, I should like to put on record some observations made on the patas monkey (*Erythrocebus*). My wife and I spent some time living away from the towns in Northern Nigeria and acquired, at separate times, a male and a female of this species. We kept these from their being very young until about nine months later. They lived, by their own choice, in practically a wild state while making use of our hut when they wanted to, especially for play. They always slept, however, in various trees in the vicinity.

Relevant points are:

(1) Aggression: Although these monkeys would cling to us when frightened, they normally showed what I gather is the usual aggression behaviour (with mouth open and back arched) if we attempted to approach too closely. It is interesting that they showed intraspecific "aggression play" with our domestic ginger cat, engaging in wrestling bouts as if all were the same species.

(2) Muteness: These monkeys often did make various noises under provocation, and occasionally as a means of communication. An example is the occasion when the male fell in a drum of water and the other shrieked loudly until he was saved.

(3) With reference to the species sleeping in isolation, we observed that in this case the pair always slept close together on a branch, usually with their arms interlocked. This is possibly related to their being still immature when we had to leave them, or to the unnatural conditions, although they lived as free a life as possible.

I wonder if Professor Hall has any comments on these points?

HALL: (1) Aggression of patas: they have a repertoire of attack-threat behaviour patterns which has some basic similarity to that of other monkeys. However, the open mouth, or gape, as we call it, occurs both in situations where attack-intention is shown and where the animals are simply nervous or frustrated. The gape is especially prominent in the adult males in the wild when the animals are alerted—perhaps because the observer has come too close to the group.

(2) Muteness: from our laboratory group observations, we are able to distinguish at least eight types of vocalization in patas, but all except three are audible to the observer only at very close ranges. The shriek, the bark, and another variety of bark (probably equivalent to the shrill bark of rhesus and baboons), seem to be the only "carrying" calls, and these occurred exceedingly rarely in the wild.

(3) Night-resting: it is obviously possible that, for example, pairs of patas in the wild would sleep close together, as do the mothers and infants, but these are minor variants in the overall dispersal pattern which was typical *of that habitat region* (Uganda).

CULLEN: Dr. Lorenz suggested that redirected attacks, aroused by the presence of the mate but orientated towards outside birds, might have a strong pair-bonding function in some species and also serve to keep away potential trespassers. Such a function might explain the puzzling lack of sexual dimorphism in those species where the male does most of the defence of the territory, where one might expect that the female's colouration would become as different as possible from the male's in order to *avoid* arousing his aggression towards her. If this idea is correct, one might expect it to apply mainly in species where neighbouring pairs are within sight of each other, for if neighbours are too far apart, there would be no nearby object to focus the redirected aggression.

LORENZ: I agree that being not too dimorphic may help territory defence, as the mates of a pair are interchangeable without effecting a great change in the stimulus situation presented to the hostile neighbour. However, I believe that the main selection pressure favouring monomorphism is schooling and flocking in birds and fishes. In birds, sexual releasers are, to a great part, so constructed that they become less conspicuous when the bird is on the wing, while the releasers of flocking, for example the wing and tail patterns that become visible only in flight, are markedly less dimorphic than most others. In fish, practically all schooling species are monomorphic, extreme sexual dimorphism is found in fish only occurs in forms that lead a sedentary life and never school. In those Cichlids which are alternately territorial and schooling, sexual dimorphism of colour is only shown in the territorial phase.

HUXLEY: Lack, Peter Scott, and others have shown that sexual dimorphism in normally dimorphic species is often lost on oceanic islands. Of course in many types, e.g. herons, grebes, divers, etc., there is no striking sexual dimorphism at all, and display is mutual. This appears to be correlated with the mode of life of the types.

LORENZ: It is certainly true that in ducks the highly differentiated nuptial plumage of the males seems to function largely as a barrier against hybridization. We know of three cases, in which a species with male nuptial colour was blown to an island, on which no other ducks occur, the Gadwall (*Anas stropera*) to Coues' island, the mallard (*Anas platyrhynchos*) to Hawaii and the pintail (*Anas acuta*) to the Kerguelen Islands. In all three cases, the sexual dimorphism all but disappeared. In the South Georgian pintail, *Anas georgica spinicauda*, it has disappeared altogether, the male being completely female-coloured. However, the species still possesses the genes for the nuptial plumage as found in *acuta*, as we recently discovered. Hybrids between *spinicauda* and *platyrhynchos* are sexually dimorphic and show a patterning intermediate not between *spinicauda* and *platyrhynchous*, but between *acuta* and *platyrhynchos*!

INTRODUCTION TO HOSTILITY IN SMALL GROUPS

By

THELMA VENESS

Psychology Department, Birkbeck College, London, England

Owing to the illness of Dr. de Monchaux, her paper which appears was distributed, but in her absence, Thelma Veness made the following contribution to the symposium.

I SUPPOSE it is to be expected that it is the first paper on *human* behaviour in this Symposium which is the first to face from the outset the semantic issues involved in the title of the Symposium. Biologists, by and large, behave as if they know what they mean by "aggression" when studying animal behaviour, whereas psychologists are still rather tentative about terminology; which is not surprising in view of the greater complexity and greater variety of the behaviour they must seek to describe. Yet questions about whether or not it is valid to speak of primary aggressiveness, even in animals, cannot begin to be answered until the discussants enter into several agreements about definitions. However, I do not want to suggest that these decisions can easily be reached. On the contrary, so far as human behaviour is concerned, I will argue that the lack of terminological exactitude is precisely because of the absence of discrete "essences" of behaviour to which different names can readily be assigned.

I do not intend to put forward a comprehensive glossary for use in discussing aggression. I do want to draw attention, however, to the manner in which Dr. de Monchaux opens her paper. Without fuss, she tells of the apparently somewhat anarchistic decision she has made: "I have used the term 'hostility' in my title, instead of aggression, in order to direct discussion towards the theme of animosity rather than of assertiveness". She is referring to the undoubted fact that technical psychological discussions, no less than lay discourse, do sometimes use the word "aggression" in contexts where it is equivalent to assertiveness or dominance over others: and furthermore, that it is used to refer to assertiveness where there is no direct implication of social interaction. For example, a man may be said to have an aggressive personality if he is generally energetic and determined in adopting and pursuing goals and if he is not easily daunted by obstacles of any kind. "Assertive" so used is virtually equivalent to "active", and some psychologists have attempted to rescue us from this sort of confusion, when describing personality traits, by adopting terms like "ascendant" and "surgent" to refer to the disposition to be assertive.

Dr. de Monchaux explains, however, that she does *not* want to be concerned with assertiveness, and so she uses the term "hostility". Now what connotations does this term have? I am not, of course, in a position to expound the connotations it has for Dr. de Monchaux. But Arnold Buss, in his book *The Psychology of Aggression* also finds the term "hostility" useful. As a matter of fact, he makes a distinction between "aggression" and "hostility", which clearly Dr. de Monchaux would not want to do; but it is worth considering this distinction to emphasize the status of "hostility" for him.

Aggression, for Buss, is "a response that delivers noxious stimuli to another organism" (p. 1). It is a response, an "instrumental response": he explicitly avoids defining it by reference to intent. Hostility, on the other hand, is an attitude. It is an "implicit verbal response involving negative feelings (ill will) and negative evaluations of people and events" (p. 12). ("Anger" is a third concept Buss uses, but this is not needed here). Now the point about saying that hostility is an "attitude" is to indicate that it is far from being a single act or sequence of acts. An attitudinal response is one that *endures*. Newcomb, too, in the paper on autistic hostility to which Dr. de Monchaux refers, calls "hostility" a "persistent attitude". A point that Buss makes should perhaps be noted—that on his definition a response can be hostile without being aggressive. Thus, a chap who goes around for weeks muttering "I hate him", well out of earshot of the "victim", need have no intention to deliver noxious stimuli, let alone actually be doing so. (But that is possibly the whole point of the "autistic hostility" to which Dr. de Monchaux devotes much of her paper—that one withdraws to a distance where one is safely out of harm's way: that is, out of the way of the harm one might *do*, rather than the harm one might receive.)

Another point about defining "hostility" as an attitude is that an attitude involves both stimulus and response generalization, both to a degree perhaps not found in other animals. Human hostile behaviour is not evoked solely by a specific releaser pattern of behaviour in the victim: indeed, the victim's soft answer that turneth away wrath may in fact have quite the opposite effect, and exacerbate the hostility yet further: "Why doesn't the wretch hit back?" may be the "implicit verbal response". Moreover, the hostility persists, as Dr. de Monchaux shows, even when the victim is not physically present. And it is a very wide variety of response that is subsumed by the term "hostility". It is surprising how hostile a smile or a gift can be; rather more directly aggressive, possibly, than sticking pins in a wax model.

Dr. de Monchaux has described how hostility may originate in unexpressed aggression, but of course this is not the only source of hostility. It can also be a by-product of *expressed* aggression, particularly when such aggression has frequently been evoked by the victim. It is not difficult to imagine persistent hostility springing from situations like those in which aggression is evoked in animals —sexual and territorial rivalry, competition for scarce resources. The situations may be similar for animal and human being, but that does not preclude the possibility of the response being entirely human. Animals may rarely "do to death", as we have frequently been told in this Symposium, but surely human beings too have found alternatives. That hostility is confined to *homo sapiens* is implied by Buss's definition, in that he makes reference to "implicit *verbal* response".

I would suggest, however, that there is another component in this process of responding to attack with hostility, which may also be entirely human, and if so, it too probably owes much to human powers of language. This component is human concern with "identity". There is a special sense in which an "overpopulation" situation applies to human existence—that there just never seems to be room for all the "selves" seeking for establishment and recognition. And so it will happen in human affairs that hostile behaviour, not just aggressive acts, can accompany the most intimate of relationships, when sexual commerce will not for long quieten a persistent assertion of selfhood which may owe nothing in itself to sexuality. This is not autistic hostility now, but Dr. de Monchaux does not concentrate exclusively on autistic forms of hostility. Indeed, far from there being withdrawal and alienation, there may be a symbiotic relationship, in which mutual hostility may have originated from self-assertion, but may then have become an indispensable means of expressing the identities of the partners: each would be lost without the object of the resentment.

But you see where I have been taken. Starting from Dr. de Monchaux's desire not to be concerned with assertiveness, and decision therefore to use the term "hostility" instead of aggression, I have arrived at the position of declaring that assertiveness is an essential component of persistent attitudes like hostility—the assertion of one's own identity. In the case of autistic hostility, withdrawal has in part this function since, as Dr. de Monchaux points out, withdrawal preserves the attitude unchanged, and doubtless to some degree the "self" is identified by the attitude. This is by no means the only important component of hostility. But the point I wished to establish was that it is by no means easy to isolate and classify the forms of human aggressive behaviour, and so to be tidy and clear-cut about terms.

Small Group Research

Dr. de Monchaux has made it clear that in small groups, the relationship between the positive feelings and behaviour of "group cohesion" and the experience and expression of aggression is by no means obvious or unambiguous. She has described "small groups", which provide the experimental material of her paper, in the simplest and most helpful way possible—by indicating the limits on the numbers of individuals involved. This feature of size is probably the only one common to all the studies known as "small group studies". It has been claimed that the special value of this kind of study is that a group is the meeting point of individual personality, social interaction phenomena and the forces of the wider culture in which the group is found: "The study of small groups is thus a method for the study of social systems, of culture, and of personality —all three." (Hare *et al.*, 1955, v.) But it is by no means the aim of every small group study—indeed perhaps not of any—to study these three levels in simultaneous interaction over the short period for which most experimental small groups last. The analysis of the phenomena observed can go on at any of these levels. Some experimenters are mostly interested in hypotheses linking individual behaviour and interaction situations—for example, Thibaut and Coules in the experiment Dr. de Monchaux cites. They compared two conditions of interaction between pairs of people to demonstrate that a person who directly answers aggressive behaviour is subsequently less aggressive in more oblique situations than is someone who is prevented from replying directly to attack. Some studies are more concerned with group phenomena *per se*, notably those of Bion to which Dr. de Monchaux refers, who classifies different kinds of group according to what are referred to as "basic assumptions" induced by the group's awareness of its own existence. Nor is there much homogeneity as yet about the theoretical frameworks which engender small group studies, partly because such studies have a diverse ancestry. Dr. de Monchaux's own interests, possibly, have led her to turn quite often to psycho-analytic ideas when discussing small group phenomena: although it must also be admitted that of psychological theories, the Freudian has had most to say about aggression. Moreover, small group studies have often originated from the need to test rigorously and systematically ideas culled from the observation of non-experimental groups, and these have quite often been therapeutic groups, as were those of Bion and Kräupl Taylor. But the ancestry of experimental groups includes also observational studies of delinquent gangs and of work teams. Thus, it is not difficult to imagine how attempts to understand "morale" in, say, fighting units could lead to experiments on group cohesion, like that of French which Dr. de Monchaux quotes. In this, the hunches that might have come from real-life studies were built into a careful experimental design. The reactions of groups differentiated on one variable only—degree of organization—were observed in what might be considered two "morale-testing" situations, the same for all groups: namely, the attempt to reach solutions, agreed by the group, on what were in fact insoluble problems; and the experience of being in a locked room with smoke pouring in under the door.

Small group studies have sometimes been criticized as being mere demonstrations of the obvious. Some of them are, of course; but their value depends upon where the experimenter goes from there. This method of study has the advantage of providing means of isolating quite complex phenomena and enabling them to be elicited, in future, reliably and in controllable conditions. There will then exist the basis for introducing variations and so for finding less obvious relationships. The further programme of experimentation can proceed in any of the directions mentioned earlier. In principle, any commonplace concerning human aggression which can be set up in a manipulable small group situation can then be further explored in any one of these directions:

(1) Further study can remain at the level of regarding the phenomenon as a social interaction pattern, but systematic variations of the basic demonstration can be introduced. There can be no doubt that the patterns of hostility that Dr. de Monchaux describes are "real" phenomena in our day-to-day interactions. But we may have notions about how to eliminate them, or attenuate their effects, notions which can first be tried out in miniature in further small group studies. Such a programme of study was conducted by Sherif and his associates (1961), who eventually found that the best way of breaking down hostility and conflict between groups of boys was by setting the groups superordinate goals whose attainment was beyond the resources of any group alone. Another example is the elegant programme of experiments of Morton Deutsch (1962, also Deutsch and Krauss, 1962) designed to explore different conditions of threat in group interaction, and the differential effects they produce.

(2) The manipulation of the basic experiment can proceed in directions suggested by analysis at the level of individual differences. An example of this is the programme of Haythorn, Carter and their associates (1956a, b), on the effects of various combinations within a group of "authoritarians" and "equalitarians", as defined by means of an individually administered attitude scale.

(3) A third possibility is that the experimental variations can proceed in a direction which has closer relevance to questions concerning hostility between yet larger social units, such as nations. Direct extrapolation from small social groups to international relations would be naive indeed. However, it is likely to be the case that every individual brings into a small group certain features of the larger culture in which he shares: and most small groups studied experimentally are homogenous in this respect. But the basic experimental demonstration, once set up in a single culture, can then be repeated in different cultures. For example, Dr. de Monchaux herself has contributed to a seven-nation comparative study of ways of handling a "deviant" planted in a small group (Schachter

et al., 1954). Milgram (1961) has compared two European nations with respect to the reactions of individuals to group pressures. As yet, rather few attempts have been made to look at group behaviour cross-culturally, but it is probable that such experimental programmes would yield more convincing demonstrations of "national characteristics" than do traditional survey methods. Such comparative studies could help to reveal the variations in the perceptions, expectations and assumptions that exist among people of different cultures, and which may operate insidiously in the conference chamber.

References

Buss, A. 1961. *The Psychology of Aggression.* New York and London: Wiley.
Deutsch, M. 1962. "Co-operation and Trust: Some Theoretical Notes." In: *Nebraska Symposium on Motivation.* Univ. Nebraska Press.
Deutsch, M., and Krauss, R. M. 1962. "Studies of Bargaining." *Conflict Resolution,* 6, 52-76.
Hare, P., Borgatta, E. F., and Bales, R. F. (eds.). 1955. *Small Groups.* New York: Knopf.
Haythorn, W., *et al.* 1956a. "The Effects of Varying Combinations of Authoritarian and Equalitarian Leaders and Followers." *J. Abnorm. Soc. Psychol.,* 53, 210-219.
Haythorn, W., *et al.* 1956b. "The Behavior of Authoritarian and Equalitarian Personalities in Small Groups." *Hum. Relat.,* 9, 57-74.
Milgram, S. 1961. "Nationality and Conformity." *Scientific American,* 205, 45-52.
Schachter, S., *et al.* 1954. "Cross-cultural Experiments on Threat and Rejection." *Hum. Relat.,* 4, 403-439.
Sherif, M., *et al.* 1961. *Intergroup Conflict and Cooperation: The Robbers Cave Experiment.* Norman, Oklahoma: the University Book Exchange.

HOSTILITY IN SMALL GROUPS

By

Cecily de Monchaux

Psychology Department, University College, London, England

I HAVE used the term "hostility" in my title, instead of "aggression", in order to direct discussion towards the theme of animosity rather than of assertiveness. I also want to leave room to consider the forms of social attack which consist in withdrawal and alienation from others. By "small groups" I have in mind those ranging in size from two to, say, ten or twelve persons. I shall not be discussing the relation between small groups and the larger social institutions of which they form part, nor shall I be especially concerned with the effect which a man's hostile behaviour towards himself may have on others, although this is an important chapter of group psychology: e.g. Stengel's (1958) demonstration of the social appeal function of suicide attempts.

The issues I shall focus on have to do with the role of hostility in shaping the pattern of interaction in small groups, and the findings I shall discuss will be drawn mainly from experimental research.

Hostility is not symmetrical with affection, for it can pull in either of two opposite directions*: towards its object for attack, or away from its object for withdrawal. If *A* picks a quarrel with *B*, there are four ways *B* can act:

(1) he can turn the other cheek (answer hostility with affection, or at least with tolerant neutrality);
(2) he can return blow for blow (answer hostility with hostility);
(3) he can become cool (answer hostility with withdrawal of affection);
(4) he can leave *A* by himself (withdraw from communication, i.e. refuse him both hostility and affection).

---

*A complication which has created problems for the dualists, from Plato to Freud, who have harnessed two horses to their theoretical chariot—love and hate, libido and aggression. Is one of the horses to have two heads, or do we add a third—fear—and argue that anger without fear leads to attack-approach and anger with fear to withdrawal? We can then distinguish between two forms of ambivalence—for which there are good clinical grounds—the "love-hate x approach" combination which is manifested in depression; and the "love-hate x withdrawal" type which is seen in schizoid illness.

The first three contingencies have corresponding forms in response to an act of affection: biting the hand that feeds, returning friendship with friendship, or inhibiting aggression. But when it comes to (4), we have an example of a very frequent response to a hostile act, which has no corresponding form in response to affection, with the possible exception of the case in which a person withdraws from a loved person for the other's sake. (In its pathological form, this "love by withdrawal" is seen in the emotional inhibitions of persons whose unconscious phantasies cause them to imagine themselves a menace to others.) Hostility which leads to withdrawal and discontinuance of communication has very different effects upon subsequent sequences of interaction than approach behaviour whether positive or negative. The result is what Newcomb (1947) has called cycles of "autistic hostility" where "conditions are created in which hostile impulses develop into persistent attitudes".

A number of different factors need to be distinguished in accounting for these cycles. Firstly, if communication is cut off, whether for reasons of hostility or not, the initial situation responsible for the establishment of a given attitude is less likely to be modified than if interaction continues. The literature of ethnic and religious prejudice abounds in examples of this aspect of cognitive restriction. For instance, Deutsch and Collins (1951) compared interracial attitudes and relationships in two types of urban dwelling in U.S.A. —those in which White and Negro lodgers were housed together, and those in which they were housed separately. They found that when there was no segregation, friendly and neighbourly relationships were much more frequent; attitudes towards Negro fellowlodgers, and towards Negroes in general, were better, quite irrespective of the other social characteristics of the persons concerned (political opinions, education, religion, etc.).

Secondly, not only does the cognitive restriction imposed by lack of communication narrow the range and retard the rate of interaction in groups, but it also stimulates the delusional features of thinking to which we tend to resort when faced with uncertainty and ambiguity. When lack of information permits us but a small sample of observations of another's behaviour, we are not likely to do justice to its complexity, and will find it easier to construct simple and concrete impressions consistent with our partial knowledge and pre-existing attitudes. Thereby we save ourselves effort, and avoid the discomfort of "cognitive dissonance" (Festinger, 1962). The development of a "halo effect" is typical and is well illustrated in a study by Jones and de Charms (1957). They compared the attitude of group members to a subject whose task failure impeded the progress of the group. When the group was working under conditions where the rewards for success depended on the group's performance as a team, a subject who performed poorly was not only judged as less dependable than when rewards rested on individual merit, but he was also given negative ratings on a number of trait clusters regarding competence, motivation and like-ability. And this negative generalization occurred although the only information members had to judge him by was his task performance on one occasion (a standard one at that, since the "failing" subject was a confederate of the experimenter).

"Halo effects" and other errors of judgment compounded of emotion and ignorance are not exclusive to aggressive attitudes, nor is the third factor at work in autistic cycles. This is the "self-fulfilling prophecy" in which "a false definition of a situation evokes a new behaviour which makes the originally false conception true" (Merton, 1957). There are "virtuous" circles as well as vicious ones but the special feature of autistic hostility compared with overtly aggressive or affectionate cycles lies in the scope left by restricted communication for mistakes to be made and acted on. The "self-fulfilling prophecy" serves not only to amplify and perpetuate cycles of hostility; it may also instigate them. Lack of com-munication may be read in error as a sign of hostility, and elicit aggression and counter-aggression. Shyness thus often pro-vokes the very behaviour in reality which its victim fears in phantasy. Mistaking the lack of a positive attitude for a negative one, or over-estimating the extent of hostility in cases where this is expressed in inhibition of affection, are the more likely to occur under con-ditions of emotional arousal.* Thus Kräupl Taylor (1957) has shown that in therapeutic groups, emotional "outsiders" have three characteristics which function to perpetuate each other—unpopu-larity, inability to show feelings to group members, and ignorance of the feelings of group members towards them. In contrast, "leaders" in these groups, i.e. people of high dominance and popu-larity, while only averagely aware of their appeal to others, are highly demonstrative in showing feelings to individual group members.

Cycles of autistic hostility are maintained, not only by increase in cognitive bias, but also by the residual effects of unexpressed aggression which each incident leaves. For we cannot assume that withdrawal from communication provides the hostile person with the same degree of emotional catharsis as attack. Thibaut and Coules (1952) observed students who had been angered by another's remarks about them, but who were not permitted to reply after being provoked. When the students wrote character sketches of those who had insulted them, the content of their descriptions showed a much sharper drop in the number of positive remarks than did that of a control group who had been permitted to reply when they had been angered. Similar effects were found when the chance of reply was merely delayed by a few minutes instead of

---

*This is analogous to the inability of the dreamer to express the idea of negation. The waking thought: "lack of love" can only be represented in the dream thought: "hate"; "X is not here" by "X is there", etc. Such regression also occurs in the thinking of young children.

being completely thwarted, showing that the results were not due to secondary hostility aroused by frustrating the expression of the primary aggression.

Residual hostility may be kept alive in the individual by the operation of defence mechanisms, the effects of which have important repercussions on his interaction with others. "Projection" contributes powerfully to the maintenance of autistic cycles: the victim of hostility who withholds expression of his counter-aggression may deal with his discomfort by projecting it imaginatively back upon the aggressor, thereby amplifying the intensity of his impression of the original hostile act. The mechanism of "response displacement" commonly affords indirect outlets for hostility in groups, resulting in various symptoms of poor group morale. For instance, dissatisfied members may obliquely express hostility by their tolerance or even selection of poor leaders. Groups in which there is hostility to the leader may support those who impede his or the group's progress.

"Stimulus displacement" accounts for other distortions of hostile attitudes in groups. Dissatisfaction experienced in the social-emotional area of group life may be displaced into the task area. Thus Kelley (1951) showed that the more unpleasant a person's position in a social hierarchy, the more likely was he to communicate irrelevant content to other members and therefore to hinder progress in the group task. Scapegoating reactions, either towards members of the in-group, or directed to out-groups may also provide targets for displacement. Finally, the close relation between the maintenance of group norms and the sentiments of members towards each other means that nonconformity can provide a channel for the expression of hostile attitudes. Here both "stimulus" and "response" displacement are implicated. Members who conform closely to the norms of a group are in general more popular with their fellows than those who do not (with the exception of leaders who are sometimes permitted more freedom to deviate, and newcomers who are permitted less freedom as the price of their initiation). Nonconformity leads to unpopularity and social isolation, which reduces the scope of and biasses the conforming members' view of the deviate. Here again we have an example, as with the projection of aggressive affect, where an indirect mode of expressing hostility has secondary effects which keep the autistic cycle in existence.

If we now ask why hostility is sometimes expressed in withdrawal and sometimes directly in aggression, we must move back to the beginning of the cycle, and examine the modifying influence which positive feelings and morale have on the form in which hostility is expressed. In group psychology, this factor is usually referred to as "cohesiveness", meaning either the sentiment of mutual liking on the part of group members, or their share in a positive interest in the functions of the group task.

The relation between cohesiveness and hostility is not a simple one. Many studies have shown that indices of cohesiveness, such as feelings of identification with the group, sacrifice of individual interests, feelings of group unity, are accompanied by a high proportion of friendly behaviour of members towards one another. Correspondingly, groups constituted of initially more aggressive persons have been shown to form less cohesive groups than those composed of less aggressive members. Conversely, however, hostility may be a sign of cohesiveness, in that members may feel so safe with each other that they can be frank in their expression of hostility. French (1944), for instance, in one of the earliest small group experiments, showed that frustration and fear had very different effects on organized and unorganized groups. The "we" feeling and interdependence of members of organized groups allowed them to express much more aggression towards one another than members of unorganized groups under similar stress. That the effect of cohesiveness in freeing the expression of hostility need not wait upon the reinforcing effect of familiarity has been shown in groups where members, though quite new acquaintances, have positive expectations of one another. Thus Pepitone and Reichling (1955) conducted an experiment in which half their pairs of subjects were led to believe that they would find each other compatible and pleasant companions, while the other half were led to expect that they would be unlikely to get on well together. Under the stress of hostile provocation from the experimenter, pairs with positive anticipations were both more often and more directly expressive of hostility than those with negative expectations.

Other studies have shown that not only may the expression of hostility be dependent upon a certain degree of cohesiveness in the group, but that such expression may constitute an important phase in the development of cohesiveness. Bales (1955) investigated the behaviour of discussion groups of from 2 to 10 subjects, hitherto strangers to one another. Each group talked over a "human relations" case, in which a choice of administrative decisions had to be made to deal with the problems described. Discussion was free, and no leader was appointed by the experimenter. Bales's analysis of the patterns of communication in these discussions showed significant similarities between groups in the sequence of phases. Increases in task-oriented activity in the early part of meetings consistently gave way to an increase in social-emotional activities in the next phase. Both positive and negative emotional reactions between members increased, with negative reactions giving way to positive ones in the final or third phase. Bales sees a reparative function in this final phase: "one might expect the successfully recovering group to confirm its agreement and to release the tensions built up in its prior task efforts, repairing the damage done to its state of consensus and social integration. We note joking and laughter so frequently at the end of meetings that they might almost be taken as a signal that the group has completed what it considers

to be a task effort, and is ready for disbandment or a new problem.
This last-minute activity completes a cycle of operations involving
a successful solution both of the task problems and social-emotional
problems confronting the group".*

An increase in cohesiveness following the expression of hostility
need not always serve a reparative end. It may be that such cycles
as Bales has described are "overdetermined" and that they result
from a combination of different effects: catharsis of hostility, which
removes an impediment to approach behaviour, together with the
cognitive changes resulting from increase in information, which
prevents confusion, apathy, and boredom in the ensuing interaction.
Small group studies have so far failed to isolate these components,
however, or to weigh them against one another.

There is also the possibility that for understanding all group
cycles, more attention needs to be paid to the individual personality
traits and history of group interaction of group members. From
psycho-analytic observations we know that for some persons,
catharsis of aggression, far from smoothing their path to friendship
with others, blocks it with guilt which makes them withdraw in
self-hatred. There are others who become angry when guilty at
being hostile, and hate the objects of their hostility for making them
hostile. For others, by contrast, catharsis of aggression is followed
by exaggerated and elated positive feelings as they reward the
objects of their aggression for failing to retaliate upon them
according to their worst phantasy fears. Then there are individual
differences in the response to others' hostility: for some, the use of
the mechanism of "identification with the aggressor" leads them
to mirror and re-enact the hostile act, while for others, hostility
may excite attempts to "buy off" and propitiate the aggressor by
compliance and inhibition of sincerity.

Some interesting work on the relation between personality and
group function has been based on Bion's (1961) theory of emotional
patterns in group behaviour. He described a number of manoeuvres
("basic assumptions") which groups in phases of emotionality use
to evade the group task: dependency, fight-flight and pairing. Stock
and Thelen (1958) and their colleagues in Chicago composed groups
of individuals with a strong predisposition to use "flight" mechanisms when faced with conflict in group situations, and compared
their behaviour with "non-flight" groups. In problem-solving tasks,
"flight" groups were characterized by their quick dismissal of
problems, a narrow range of ideas, and constricted expression of
affect. Typically, "flight" members tended, when in heterogeneous
groups, to reject "pairing" members, for these offered a continual
invitation to emotional involvement. "Flight" members appeared

---

*The balance of positive and negative sentiment which leads to the use of
joking and laughter as a "hostility releaser" is a subtle one, and difficult to
specify. Bradney (1957) showed how joking relationships developed in one
industrial setting but not in another though it was similar in many respects.

to agree with, and feel safest with each other, and to select one another as their group spokesmen.

By such mechanisms, coalitions of persons may develop on the basis of similar personality or pathology, and through their investment of power in leaders* who "fit" their needs, may play a part in determining the outcomes of hostile group action far out of proportion to the summed value of their individual motives.

References

Bales, R. F. 1955. "The equilibrium problem in small groups." In P. Hare, E. F. Borgatta and R. F. Bales: *Small Groups*. New York: Knopf.

Bion, W. R. 1961. *Experiences in Groups*. London: Tavistock.

Bradney, P. 1957. "The joking relationship in industry." *Hum. Relat.*, **10**, 179-187.

Deutsch, M., and Collins, M. 1951. *Interracial Housing: a Psychological Evaluation of a Social Experiment*. Minneapolis: University of Minnesota Press.

Festinger, L. 1962. *A Theory of Cognitive Dissonance*. London: Tavistock.

French, J. R. P. 1944. "Organized and unorganized groups under fear and frustration." In K. Lewin *et al.*: *Authority and Frustration*. Iowa: University of Iowa Press.

Jones, E. E., and de Charms, R. 1957. "Changes in social perception as a function of the personal relevance of behaviour." *Sociometry*, **20**, 75-85.

Kelley, H. H. 1951. "Communication in experimentally created hierarchies." *Hum. Relat.*, **4**, 39-56.

Kräupl Taylor, F. 1957. "Display of dyadic emotions." *Hum. Relat.*, **10**, 257-262.

Merton, R. K. 1957. *Social Theory and Social Structure*. Glencoe: Free Press.

Newcomb, T. M. 1947. "Autistic hostility and social reality." *Hum. Relat.*, **1**, 3-20.

Pepitone, A., and Reichling, G. 1955. "Group cohesiveness and the expression of hostility." *Hum. Relat.*, **8**, 327-37.

Stengel, E., and Cook, N. G. 1958. *Attempted Suicide*. London: Chapman and Hall.

Stock, D., and Thelen, H. A. 1958. *Emotional Dynamics and Group Culture*. New York: University Press.

Thibaut, J. W., and Coules, J. 1952. "The role of communication in the reduction of interpersonal hostility." *J. abnorm. soc. Psychol.*, **47**, 770-7.

---

*Bion (1961): "The leader on the basic-assumption (emotionality) level, does not create the group by virtue of his fanatical adherence to an idea, but is rather the individual whose personality renders him peculiarly susceptible to the obliteration of individuality by the basic-assumption group's leadership requirements. . . . Thus the leader in the fight-flight group, for example, appears to have a distinctive personality because his personality is of a kind that lends itself to exploitation by the group demand for a leader who requires of it only a capacity for fighting or for flight; the leader has no greater freedom to be himself than any other member of the group."

AGGRESSION AND MENTAL ILLNESS

By

DENIS HILL

Middlesex Hospital Medical School, London, England

THE natural history of aggression, in so far as the phenomena of mental illness throw any light upon it, cannot be discussed without reference to the two main sources of theory concerning the nature of aggression. The first of these is the dual instinct theory of Freud (1949) which conceives the individual as genetically endowed with a given amount or quantum of energy directed towards destructiveness in the widest sense and which must inevitably be expressed in some form or another. If blocked or inhibited in its direct external manifestation, it pursues a more indirect pathway or if prevented from external expression altogether, turns back upon the individual himself and may destroy him. This theory expressed in a modern form by Toman (1960) conceives aggression as an aspect of desires which are biologically primitive. "The more primitive desires or the more primitive forms of satisfying given desires, are also more aggressive or destructive." In the course of individual development the primitiveness, and hence the aggressiveness of desires, diminishes, but at the same time behaviour to implement aggressive desires becomes more efficient and also more varied and complex. If aggressive desires are not acted upon, counter-cathexis or defence against them occurs. This is conceived as a process of "unlearning" of forms of behaviour which no longer satisfy such desires, and their replacement by other forms of behaviour. These may be biologically useful and socially acceptable or they may not. Whatever the consequence, however, such substitute forms of behaviour have the function of diminishing anxiety for the individual. Anxiety and aggression within this general theory are regarded as "twin brothers". The more primitive the desires, the greater the aggressiveness, and the greater the anxiety. "Anxiety is a state of the psyche in which more primitive, hence aggressive, desires than usual prevail" (Toman, 1960). The economic aspect of all psychological theories of this type must be emphasized. If the first outflow of energy is blocked by frustration, the energy is not lost but remains to be deflected one way or another and the forms of its expression may or may not be healthy for the individual himself or the society in which he lives.

The second group of theories regarding the nature of aggression stem from the work of Dollard *et al.* (1939) and conceive aggression, not as an inherent genetically given quantum of energy seeking expression but rather as a by-product of frustration, initially the invariable response to it. Since in our species frustration of basic drives is universal, aggressive responses at the start of life are also universal. In this theory the strength of the tendency to aggressive behaviour varies with the amount of frustration, and there is experimental evidence to support this. But the aggressive responses to frustration are themselves subject to frustration and are met in the upbringing of most human infants with punishment and pain, rather than rewards. The inhibition therefore of any act of aggression depends upon the amount of anticipated pain and punishment which would follow if the act were not inhibited. The effects of frustration in animals and human infants and children have been the subject of considerable research, both experimental and observational. The ways in which the maturing child learns to acquire forms of behaviour which are gratifying, rewarding and socially acceptable and avoids forms of behaviour which bring punishment and pain are the subject matter of all developmental psychology.

The study of man and particularly of the mentally ill provides us every day with experience of the truth that under conditions of frustration one of three things can happen as a result of the aggression aroused. It may be directed overtly at the frustrator or frustrating circumstance in the form of anger, verbal hostility or physical violence; it may suffer displacement on to a non-aggressor or inanimate object (the scapegoat) or it may be inhibited with possible adverse consequences for the person frustrated. The choice of pathway for the aggression aroused, if we care to look at it like that, is determined by a great variety of complex factors, not only involving past personal experience, i.e. learning, and innate and acquired constitutional factors in the personality of the individual, but also the occasion, the social milieu and the cultural norms of the society in which the individual lives.

The Effect of Cerebral Disease

A common workaday hypothesis with which most psychiatrists work is that mental breakdown, whether it be in the form of neurotic illness, psychotic break with reality or acting out in antisocial psychopathic behaviour is brought about as a consequence of mounting emotional tension, the causes of which may be complex, varied, specific to the individual but are always multiple. Emotional tension is unpleasant, involves anxiety and conflict of motives and becomes of such severity that the patient feels hopeless and helpless. Frustration of needs with consequent arousal of aggression and all the countering forces to control it are always present. There can be no doubt that there is great individual variability in our tolerance to suffer this state of affairs, of the extent to which we can control aggressive feelings, inhibit them without destroying ourselves or becoming ill. It is therefore of interest to consider the effects of brain disease and of brain maturation on this process. Little is known about the latter.

An early observation made after the pandemic of encephalitis lethargica in 1920 was the profound alteration of conduct which often followed recovery from the disease. Within a few months, particularly in children aged from three to ten years, a marked destructiveness and impulsiveness often ensued. Primitive aggressive and sexual impulses were immediately carried into action, with consequent serious and even murderous attacks on others, but occasionally upon themselves leading to gruesome self-mutilation. Children who had previously been normally behaved would lie, steal, destroy property, set fire and commit various sexual offences, without thought of punishment. Yet subsequently they seemed to retain the capacity for remorse (Brill, 1959). All over the world special institutions were set aside for the care and protection of these children. The brain areas chiefly affected by this disease are the basal ganglia, hypothalamus and the periaqueductal grey matter of the brain stem, but it has never proved possible to relate focal pathology to specific forms of conduct disorder. In recent years, however, more light has been thrown on this, both from experimental studies on animals, starting with the work of Bard (1928) and that of Klüver and Bucy (1939) and from observing the effects of brain lesions in man and their surgical removal. Animal work, however, has by now made it clear that particular cerebral systems are concerned with adaptive behaviour when the animal is aroused by a "motivational requirement" to use a physiologist's word, or a "need" or "drive" to use psychologists' words. These areas, known as the limbic system or "visceral brain" are found in the old rhinencephalon or smell brain and occupy the hilus of each cerebral hemisphere, a part of the brain in which phylogenetically old and new cortex meet. The contradictory results of electrical stimulation and of the placing of surgical lesions in these parts of the brain of rats, cats and monkeys indicate that there must be species differences. Lesions in one area in one species may produce a docile unaggressive animal and in another a wildly ferocious beast with a low threshold for the eliciting of rage reactions. Olds and Milner (1954) have shown that within this limbic system there are areas which when electrically stimulated can be used as reinforcement stimuli for learning in the rat. Moreover when electrodes are left implanted in the freely moving animal, it can learn to reward itself by pressing a lever which makes the circuit to provide the self-stimulation. Olds has shown that electrical self-stimulation by the rat of its own limbic system is as strong a reward as the obtaining of food is for the hungry animal. It is of interest that the points from which rewarding self-stimulation in the brain were found to be numerous, those producing the opposite effect—a non-reinforcement in a learning situation, which is the equivalent of punishment perhaps, are very few and far between. There is evidence in Old's view (1958) that there are different parts of the limbic system which are differentially affected by certain needs of the organism. Under the influence of a need a given area will elicit a complex pattern of adaptive behaviour aimed at bringing about satisfaction of the need. This it does through bringing into play both automatic inborn responses in the autonomic nervous system and the endocrine system and also less automatic and previously learned responses through the musculo-skeletal system. The outlets for the limbic system are through the hypothalamus and brain-stem reticular system on the one hand, and probably the hypothalamic-pituitary connections on the other.

For some years it has been known that both adequate electrical stimulation and the placing of discrete surgical lesions will greatly modify an animal's aggression-threshold in a variety of species. Over thirty years ago Bard (1928) showed that the cat with "sham rage"—a phenomenon known in decorticate dogs for more than sixty years, must have the caudal part of the hypothalamus intact. These animals show great sympathetic stimulation, with erect hair, dilated pupils, racing heart and snarling, and lashing of the tail —all signs of rage, but may at the same time lap milk. There is, therefore, an inborn mechanism for the eliciting of aggressive behaviour and it seems probable that this lies caudally in the limbic system, the more cephalic portions of which exercise an inhibitory function over it—as indeed the cerebral cortex does.

When we turn to the observations on human patients whose brains have altered either by surgery or who have focal cerebral disease, the findings are much what we would expect. A low threshold for aggressive behaviour, intolerance of frustration, impulsiveness and irritability and a variety of disorders of personality are found in about 50 per cent of patients with lesions either in or impinging upon the limbic system. This is particularly evident in that group of patients with "temporal lobe epilepsy" in which focal brain lesions are found in the depths of the temporal lobe—the amygdala—uncal—hippocampal areas. Lesions here, whether atrophic due to interference with blood supply, or neoplastic can transform the personality. This occurs whether epilepsy results or not. A common example of this disease is that which starts in childhood due probably to atrophic lesions in the rhinencephalon, acquired through a difficult birth. These children often present a serious behaviour problem, due to their chronic dissatisfaction, their impulsive irritability and bad temper, their egotism and failure to learn by experience. Later, mood changes with anxiety or depression and almost any form of neurotic behaviour or sexual perversion may occur. In adult life psychosis results in about a quarter of the patients, either a severe depression or a paranoid illness with hallucinations and ideas of persecution, resembling schizophrenia.

While aggressive change of personality is less common following lesions in man in other parts of the limbic system, this has been described following acute destruction in the medial frontal cortex which is close to the cingulate gyrus, in the orbital cortex of the frontal lobe and in the anterior hypothalamus. Mention here must also be made of the effects of surgery carried out for the relief of mental illness—the so-called psychosurgical procedures. Jacobsen (1936) had shown that chimpanzees following surgical interference with the cortex of both frontal lobes showed a markedly raised tolerance of frustration and no rage responses occurred in a situation the object of which was to provoke a neurosis. In the human leucotomy the connections severed are those afferent to the frontal cortex from the thalamus, part of the excitation from which thereafter fails to reach the cortex. As a result patients become less anxious, less concerned with their inner experience and more concerned with the environment. The effects on aggressive behaviour are interesting. Self-directed violence in the form of suicide, mutilation or starvation yields better to the operation than externally directed violence, such as irritability, belligerence and defiance (Freeman, 1959). In fact assaultiveness in a psychotic or psychopathic patient has always been a contraindication to this surgical procedure.

The Effect of Age

The overt expression of aggressive behaviour is probably at maximal potential at the start of life, is reduced during later childhood and re-emerges to lesser degree during adolescence, thereafter to decline. The temper-tantrums of the normal five-year-old are not seen again, unless the brain is seriously diseased in later life by senile atrophy or arteriosclerosis and even then there is rarely much violence. Cerebral disease and serious head injury in childhood are particularly liable to be followed by irritability, violent temper, fighting behaviour and unmanageableness. Antisocial behaviour with lying, stealing and destructiveness are common. Unlike the postencephalitic cases, these patients tend to improve with the passage of time. In adult life the proportion of the population showing overtly aggressive or destructive behaviour as a result of mental illness compared with the proportion of emotionally sick children who do, is very small. Indeed "acting-out" behaviour disorders in children would seem much commoner than the children who are brought to the psychiatrist with symptoms of depression, anxiety or manifest emotional upheaval. In childhood, the methods of dealing with frustration and the arousal of aggression are immature, the countering measures poorly developed and in particular inhibition and withdrawal, often seen in the adult are rare except in the seriously ill child. An example of displacement activity, the paranoid mechanism, is extremely rare before puberty. An important exception to the general rule that the overt manifestations of aggressive behaviour in the mentally ill decline with age

is the case of the psychopathic disorders, that group of patients
whose abnormality becomes manifest at puberty or early adolescence.
These patients whose behaviour is dominated by their desires, called
"instinct-ridden" characters, act upon their needs and frustrations
without consideration for others. Lacking a sense of guilt, they are
immune to anxiety and stresses and do not learn from punishment.
All form of antisocial behaviour including dangerous assaults,
sexual aggressiveness and even murder occur. About 10 per cent
of murderers are probably in this category. It is of interest that the
pattern of the spontaneous electrical activity of the cerebral cortex
of aggressive psychopaths is often an immature one resembling the
patterns of childhood. The incidence of such immature E.E.G.'s
in psychopaths, however, declines with advancing age as does too
the violence of their behaviour. Given time the aggressive psychopath becomes amenable.

Aggression Turned on the Self

There are wide implications which follow upon the idea that
aggression, thwarted of direct expression by counter forces within
the personality and not being directed elsewhere in "scapegoat"
activity, can turn upon the self. The phenomenon is generally
accepted by psychopathologists and ethologists have provided
examples from animal and bird behaviour which are more than
analogous. Self-destructive behaviour, both literal and by implication, is very common in many forms of mental illness. The most
obvious example of this is witnessed every day in patients with
severe depression in whom the central preoccupation is of a self-
reproachful nature and may be supported by a range of delusional
ideas about the enormity of past sins or the essential worthlessness
of the self. In another type self-destructiveness takes the forms of
delusional belief of having incurable disease, cancer and so on. In
depression the patient accuses himself of acts and attitudes for which
he really blames someone else. Suicide is the final act of aggression
turned on the self, and of course is not rare in depressive illness.
It is commoner as age advances, four times as frequent in men than
women, and the peak age in most countries is in the age group over
seventy years. Unsuccessful suicidal attempts are commoner in
women than men. The majority of such patients are either mentally
ill or immature personalities in a situation of emotional conflict.
Many unsuccessful attempts are made by people in a state of
impulsive and uncontrolled rage (Yap, 1958).

How far the mechanism of aggression turned on the self can be
taken is disputed. There are considerable numbers of persons with
odd asocial characters whose lives can be seen to be dominated by
moral masochism, by harmful self-abnegation, by ascetism carried
to the point at which physical malnutrition supervenes, but in these
cases there is often evidence that the activities are pleasurable and
emotionally rewarding. The drives with which these people are

coping are perhaps more often sexual ones. It is, however, a common-place that many neurotic persons appear repeatedly to show behaviour which is ultimately not in their best interests, to make foolish errors of judgement which inevitably and predictably lead to their own unhappiness. Much petty crime involves behaviour ensuring the certainty of detection and hence the inevitability of punishment. Dermatitis artefacta, a condition most commonly seen among neurotic adolescent girls involving self-excoriation and mutilation of the skin, often of the face with consequent loss of attractiveness, develops usually in a situation involving stress, unexpressed hostility and guilt feelings. Psychogenic pain, felt in a limb or discrete area of the body, often develops in a setting of depression and intense hostility towards someone loved but on whom the patient is dependent emotionally. It would seem that the law of Talion operates; to the extent that the patient wishes to cause the loved person to suffer pain, to that extent he must suffer pain himself. These issues and many others are discussed in Karl Menninger's well-known book *Man Against Himself*.

Displacement of Aggression

The prototype of displacement of aggression is of course the selection of a "scapegoat". This may be another unoffending individual, an institution, a system of ideas or beliefs or an inanimate object. In episodes of rage, disturbed children, psychopathic and psychotic adults engage in apparently meaningless destruction, commit arson or attack people on brief acquaintance and with minimal provocation. Alcoholism in the psychopathic patient is a common precipitant. Displacement is also seen as a mental mechanism in the production of symptoms in other groups of patients. It is an essential defensive manoeuvre in obsessional and paranoid illnesses. In the former, objects, places or ideas are invested with danger, are phobically avoided and rituals are de-veloped to maintain the avoidance. In the latter, intense suspicion and ideas of persecution are entertained about known or unknown persons who are felt to be dangerous and out to harm or destroy the patient. As already mentioned paranoid symptoms are very rare in childhood. Their incidence in all mental illnesses increases with advancing age.

Inhibition and Withdrawal

In the face of strong counter-forces within the personality to the expression of aggressive and sexual drives, in the absence of sub-stitute methods for their expression, either healthy, neurotic or perverse, and usually in the presence of an unfavourable environ-ment, inhibition and withdrawal may occur. It is commonly held that schizophrenia is the prototype mental illness in which this process is witnessed. There are, however, many eccentric non-psychotic individuals who withdraw from contact with their fellows and lead lives as recluses. In schizophrenia the desires and impulses which cannot be realised in actuality are carried on in phantasy and an extreme introverted day-dreaming. The phantasies and even delusional ideas about omniscience and omnipotence, about world destruction and annihilation are evidence that aggressiveness has not been lost. Occasionally, however, such impulses suddenly escape control and the mute almost stuporose patient commits a sudden act of minor or major violence. Owing to changed attitudes to the mentally ill and modern pharmacological treatments, these episodes are now rare. Chronic schizophrenics, however, are unhappily still with us, and it is not rare to meet in the chronic wards of large psychiatric hospitals, partially deteriorated patients of the paranoid type who, while relating very poorly to their human environment, meet all-comers with intense hostility and a stream of incoherent verbal abuse.

The Environment

For centuries the mentally ill were regarded as all potentially dangerous and morally bad. They were treated with the greatest brutality and cruelty and were in fact one of the groups of scapegoats for an aggressive, frightened and insecure society. The history of the treatment of the mentally ill (e.g. Zilboorg, 1941) is a horrific story and some of the harshness, the fears and the hostility to them has reached into the present time. Dungeons, chains, handcuffs, instruments of torture, straitjackets, whippings and duckings began to disappear about the time of the French Revolution, but security measures, locked doors, poor diet and paupers' clothes, and a variety of measures of restraint continued until the Second World War. Wherever they persist today they are regarded as the evils of psychiatric care. We have now learnt the lesson that to the extent to which the mentally sick are treated with aggressiveness, to that extent they have difficulties in coping with their own aggressive tendencies.

Conclusions

There can be little doubt that aggressiveness occurs as a result of frustration and that the latter is fundamental to human life. But aggressiveness is itself commonly frustrated and may then be displaced or inhibited. The study of mental illness demonstrates a variety of ways in which aggressiveness is handled. These are not unique to the mentally ill but only differ from normal functions in the intensity and severity with which they are engaged in. Since animal experimental studies have demonstrated an inherent physiological mechanism for the organization and expression of aggressive behaviour, there is support here for the theory of primacy of aggression as an innate "instinct" proposed by Freud. In this respect aggression is seen to fall in line with other drives which serve to preserve the individual and perpetuate the species. For each of them an organic organization within bodily structure can be described, and can be changed by chemical or surgical action, or by physical disease. The economic aspects of the Freudian hypothesis cannot and probably never will be validated. It may be improper to attempt to treat psychic energy in terms with which physical energy can be treated. The unbiological metapsychology of Freud which ascribed a primary destructiveness towards the self is again a cause of much confusion and is not a question which can be answered. Nevertheless self-destructive behaviour, in one form or another is a commonplace phenomenon among the mentally ill. There is some evidence that the ways of handling frustration and aggression change with increasing age. Direct overt aggression, verbal and physical is commonest in childhood and adolescence; displacement, seen particularly in the paranoid mental illnesses, becomes commonest in late middle age and the tendency to self-destruction, typified by suicide, increases as age advances, reaching a peak at the age of seventy.

References

Bard, P. 1928. "A diencephalic mechanism for the expression of rage with special reference to the sympathetic nervous system." *Amer. J. Physiol.*, **84**, 490.

Brill, H. 1959. "Postencephalitic psychiatric conditions." Chap. 56 in Vol. 2. *American Handbook of Psychiatry*. New York: Basic Books.

Dollard, J., Doob, L., Miller, N., Mowrer, O., and Sears, R. 1939. *Frustration and Aggression*. New Haven.

Freeman, W. 1959. "Psychosurgery." Chap. 76, p. 1521 in Vol. 2. *American Handbook of Psychiatry*. New York: Basic Books.

Freud, S. 1949. *An outline of psychoanalysis*. London.

Jacobsen, C. F. 1936. "Studies of cerebral function in primates." *Comp. Psychol. Monogr.*, **13**: No. 63, 3.

Klüver, H., and Bucy, P. C. 1939. "Preliminary analysis of functions of the temporal lobes in monkeys." *Arch. Neurol. Psychiat.*, 42, 979.

Olds, J., and Milner, P. 1954. "Positive reinforcement produced by electrical stimulation of septal area and other regions of rat brain." *J. Comp. Physiol. Psychol.*, 47, 419.

Olds, J. 1958. "Adaptive functions of paleocortical and related structures," in *Biological and Biochemical Bases of Behaviour*. Ed. Harlow and Woolsey. Univ. Wisconsin Press.

Toman, W. 1960. *Psychoanalytic theory of motivation*. London.

Yap, P. M. 1958. *Suicide in Hong Kong*. London.

Zilboorg, G. 1941. *A history of medical psychology*. London.

COSTUME AS A MEANS OF SOCIAL AGGRESSION

By

JAMES LAVER

Formerly Keeper of Prints and Drawings,
Victoria and Albert Museum, London, England

Homo sapiens at the moment of his emergence wore no clothes; Industrial Man in the egalitarian world of hypothetical Communism will presumably have no class distinction. But between these two points lies the whole history of fashion, a history in which distinctions of class have played a very important part. From the first, or almost from the first, there has been a distinction between clothes for use and clothes for ornament, between working clothes and fine clothes; and class distinction may be said to arise when one set of people takes to wearing fine clothes all the time and another set of people takes to wearing working clothes all the time.

The individual soon began to discover that the wearing of clothes, in however primitive a form, gave rise to certain agreeable mental reactions. They marked him out from his fellows; they enhanced the feeling of his own importance; they titillated his dawning aesthetic sense. The successful were from the first able to adorn themselves (and adorn their wives) more lavishly than the unsuccessful, and the germ of class distinction was already present. Soon it came to be taken for granted that the chief was *entitled* to more decoration than the simple warriors. In time the system crystallized first into an unwritten sumptuary law and then into the insignia of rank. This is the Hierarchical Principle which still makes it seem natural that the red band round the hat of the General is out of place round the hat of the private.

The Hierarchical Principle is therefore one of the abiding principles of dress. In the history of Fashion it has applied mostly to men, and this is because men are chiefly admired for their *position*. In primitive times this meant their strength but such a state of affairs does not last very long. The magnificent male (who is nothing else) has today sunk to the status of the gigolo, and women who admire gigolos are throw-backs to more primitive types.

With women the situation is somewhat different. In primitive times (leaving aside such complicated questions as exogamy and the like) the powerful chief chose his women at least in part for their sexual attractiveness, and for the greater part of social history this has continued to be the case. In women, therefore, the Hierarchical Principle is expressed in another form which we may call the Seduction Principle.

There remains the Utility Principle. The importance of this element is often exaggerated, but it cannot be entirely ignored. It is the ballast in the ship, or rather the counterweight to the two other principles, the Hierarchical Principle in the case of men, the Seduction Principle in the case of women. Male dress, throughout most of its history, follows the Hierarchical Principle slightly modified by the Utility Principle. However, although the role of the Seduction Principle is reduced to very small proportions, it is not entirely absent.

All male costume tends to become a uniform, by which is meant not something which is worn by everyone, but something that can be worn only by certain people. Once any kind of civilization has been established we find a whole system of uniforms. The King has a special dress, so has the Priest. In this sense, the dress of all men of a certain social rank is a uniform. When Europe emerged from the Dark Ages we find that those who could afford them wore what it is convenient to call "aristocratic" clothes. Such clothes were, in the first place, extremely rich and they became more so after the Crusades had opened up trade with the East. Silks, brocades, damasks (the very word damask is an indication of where such materials originally came from) became available to those who could afford them, and the wearing of clothes made of them was an assertion of status, i.e. a means of social aggression.

However, with the growing wealth of cities and the emergence of a prosperous trading class a new complication arose. Mere wealth without (as yet) any corresponding status faced the aristocracy with a new problem: how to prevent the wealthy bourgeois (and the wealthy bourgeoise) from dressing as gorgeously as they did themselves.

Their answer was to get the government of the day to enact sumptuary laws. Philippe le Bel in 1292 issued what is perhaps the first of these, regulating the number of the dresses and the value of the materials of which they were to be made for each different class of society. The provisions of this law are curious enough: neither man nor women of the bourgeoisie was to wear *vair*, or *gris* or ermine, nor were they allowed to wear gold, or precious stones, or crowns of gold or silver. The ladies of dukes, of earls, or of barons of six thousand livres of land or more, might have four new robes a year and no more. The same regulation applied to the other sex. Knights, and of course their ladies, were allowed two robes a year, either by gift, or purchase, or otherwise. No damoiselle, unless she were a chatelaine, or a lady of two thousand livres of land, was to have more than one robe a year. Limits were also placed on the value of materials. The wives of barons were not to have a robe of material worth more, according to the value in Paris, of 25 sols tournois a yard; the wives of bannerets and chatelains were limited to 18 sols a yard; and the wives of bourgeois of the worth of 2,000 livres tournois or more were limited to 16 sols a yard; and the poorer class to 12 sols.

This attitude received a good deal of support from moralists who objected on religious grounds to all finery but felt compelled to make some exception in the case of the upper classes. Even the sour Puritan, Philip Stubbes, writing in the reign of Elizabeth, feels constrained to add to his diatribes against vanity in dress the following significant passage:

"I doubt not but it is lawful for the nobility, the gentry, and the magistery to wear rich attire, everyone in their calling. The nobility and gentry to enoble, garnish and set forth their births, dignities and estates. The magistrates to dignify their callings, and to demonstrate the excellence, the majesty and the worthiness of their offices and functions, thereby to strike a terror and fear into the hearts of the people, to offend against their office and authority . . . and as for private subjects, it is not at any hand lawful that they should wear silks, velvets, satins, damasks, gold, silver, and what they list (though they be never so able to maintain it), except they, being in some kind of office in the Commonwealth, do use it for the dignifying and ennobling of the same . . . but now there is such a confused mingle-mangle of apparel and such preposterous excess thereof, as everyone is permitted to flaunt it out in what apparel he lusteth himself, or can get by any kind of means. So that it is very hard to know who is noble, who is worshipful, who is a gentleman, who is not; for you shall have those who are neither of the nobility, gentility, nor yeomanry, no, nor yet any magistrate or officer in the Commonwealth, go daily in silks, velvets, satins, damasks, taffetta, and such like, notwithstanding that they be both base by birth, mean by estate, and servile by calling, and this is a great confusion and a general disorder in a Christian Commonwealth."

I need not remind you that "every attempt to guide, control, or modify the freedom of fashion has been a signal failure. The only laws that have never had a shade of success, that have always been obliged to withdraw their pretentions and have become dead letters in the statute book almost before the ink had dried in which they were written, have been sumptuary laws . . . fashion has always been stronger than legislation".

The men and women of the Middle Classes continued to ape the aristocracy and sometimes even to outdo them in finery. The real distinction was between those engaged in manual toil and those who were not. Aristocratic clothes say, "I do not work". The desire for protection against the elements and ease in working is of course operative among the working classes of all periods. Among the upper classes it has often been inverted to become the Anti-Utility Principle. So soon as upper class male costume ceases to be actively military it is designed to show that if the wearer is not fighting, he is certainly not working.

The beginning of this tendency can be seen in the fantastic male clothes of the fifteenth century, but it reaches its most interesting development in the sixteenth in the form of a symbol. Clean linen round the neck is a sign still that the wearer does not engage in manual toil. We still wear clean linen at wrist and throat—that is to say the two places in which it is most easily dirtied—in order to show that we do not engage in manual toil. The ruff of the Tudor period was a fantastic exaggeration of this idea. Some of the ruffs were so huge that it must have been difficult for the wearers to feed themselves. The ruff, in fact, served the same purpose as the long finger nails of the Chinese Mandarin. It was the mark especially of the courtier, and courtier costume may be said to dominate male fashion until the end of the *Ancien Régime* in France at the close of the eighteenth century.

That revolt of the *Grande Bourgeoisie* which is called the French Revolution displaced the courtier and with him the distinction between the nobleman and the ordinary gentleman. This, of course, was not the victory of democracy but the triumph of gentility.

Gentility has been defined as a conspiracy against the aristocracy. It succeeded in getting it generally accepted that there were in practice only two classes: gentlefolk and the rest. Any man above a certain social level who conformed to certain rules and tabus was a gentleman. A duke was no more and in the nineteenth century would not have dared to wear his star and garter in the street as he would have done without question a hundred years before. Gentility meant plain clothes (the plainer the better), and gentlemen no longer prided themselves on the flowers and braiding on their sleeves but on the tailor's name inside one of the pockets.

The men who made the French Revolution had an enormous admiration for all things English and nineteenth century male dress originally derived from the clothes of the English country gentleman in the second half of the eighteenth. The tall hat is essentially a riding hat (it might even be called a primitive crash helmet), the cut-away tail coat is a riding coat. What every man above a certain social level was trying to say throughout the nineteenth century was: "I am an English country gentleman; I ride horses". So strong was the pressure of the time that the same costume was adopted even below the level of gentility, and the sensible working clothes of the lower orders frequently abandoned. The class distinction upon which the idea of gentility insisted became a very subtle matter of style and cut and small distinguishing marks. Men's clothes were none the less founded on the Hierarchical Principle, however toned down and modified by gentility and "good form". They still continued to say "I do not work". As Thorsten Veblen remarks in his *The Theory of the Leisured Class:* "Much of the charm that invests the patent leather shoe, the stainless linen, the lustrous cylindrical hat and the walking stick, that so greatly enhance the natural dignity of a gentleman comes of their pointedly suggesting that the wearer cannot when so attired bear a hand in any employment that is directly or immediately of any human use". The type of gentleman described by Veblen is now extinct. But the Principle continues to operate. That "gentility" in clothes is a less obvious kind of social aggression than "aristocracy" in clothes is obvious; it is none the less real.

We have already noted that all men's clothes tend to become a uniform. They undergo a process of fossilization which tends to make them less and less comfortable. But even gentlemen desire to engage in some active pursuits so long as they can be cleared of the stigma of work. Any active pursuit which is free from this stigma is known as sport.

We have already seen that the clothes of the eighteenth century French courtier were replaced by the clothes of the English country gentleman and these clothes were originally reasonably comfortable. But they gradually became tighter and more formal and, by the middle of the nineteenth century, the old cutaway coat had become an evening coat rigid in form and black in colour. No further evolution was possible, and just as the eighteenth century noble-man's clothes had now become servants' dress (the powdered foot-man) so the tail coat was adopted by waiters. When men required *comfortable* clothes they were compelled to bring in new country clothes. These were the check suits and billycock hats which were later to be transformed into the formal bowler and lounge suit of a more recent age. Men's clothes, in general, seem to follow an inevitable evolution; they are sports clothes, then ordinary town wear, then formal day or evening wear and finally servants' dress, after which they become mere historical curiosities.

Formerly change occurred by adopting a new sports costume as ordinary wear and the Principle still operates. But sport now no longer means only the British country pursuits which gave us first modified riding clothes and then tweeds. In the period between the world wars two new elements entered into the arena. The fashion for winter sports in Switzerland gave us the ski-ing costume, from which the modern battle dress and its civilian equivalents is derived. The vogue for Riviera holidays in the hottest part of the year brought in all kinds of informal shorts and shirts and sweaters, based on those of the fishermen of the coast. These are the new "sports clothes" whose influence will modify ordinary dress. They have clearly had an effect on American clothes which are noticeably less conventional and more comfortable than our own.

How do women fit into this picture? It is true that the clothes of queens and great ladies have been largely governed by the Hier-archical Principle, but in women's dress there is always another element, the element we have called the Seduction Principle, and it is the operation of this Principle which is properly called Fashion.

In Ancient Egypt the poorer classes and the female slaves in the palaces went about naked. The wearing of clothes was itself a class distinction, but such a system gives little scope for anything we should recognize as Fashion. The clothes of the Minoan civilization in Crete, on the other hand, are "fashionable" almost in the modern sense. The costumes of classical times are, by contrast, almost puritanical in their severity. Any attempts at exploiting the Seduction Principle seemed to have been confined to the Hetairae; and it was not until the end of the fourteenth century that the Seduction Principle found its first real flowering in the luxurious courts in France and Burgundy. It was here that *décolletage* was first discovered and exploited, here that novelty was first pursued for its own sake, and here, therefore, that true Fashion may be said to begin.

The influence of courts, however, was not all on one side. They provided a platform for Fashion but they were also rooted by their nature in the Hierarchical Principle. It is possible to study the conflict and the interaction of the two tendencies over several centuries, and the resultant forms of dress which emerged. One example may suffice. The great ruffs of the second half of the sixteenth century have already been mentioned as examples of the Hierarchical (Anti-Utility) Principle. In men this Principle was complete and the ruff a perfect round. But women were governed also by the Seduction Principle (i.e. they wanted to take advantage of the *décolletage*) and so the ruff was broken to allow the bosom to be exposed. The ruffs worn by the ladies of the court of Elizabeth show this curious compromise.

Whether the Hierarchical Principle or the Seduction Principle ruled at any given court depended largely upon the personal character of the monarch. At austere courts like that of Spain, Hierarchy became almost fossilized, with the result that the court costumes of 1600 remained unmodified almost throughout the century. When Louis XIV met his Spanish bride she was still wearing a farthingale. But at Louis's own court the Seduction Principle had won the day, since it was always possible that any lady might attract the favour of the monarch.

Fashion had begun to filter down, but the process was at first a slow one, since, until well into the eighteenth century, the wives and daughters of the bourgeoisie had work to do and so were compelled, like their poorer sisters, to dress more or less in accordance with the Utility Principle. It was not until the Industrial Revolution that the *Bourgeoise* found herself largely relieved of those duties of baking and brewing, or sewing and spinning, which had been woman's task for untold ages, and the period of middle class indolence provided a whole new world for Fashion to conquer. It is no accident that the end of the eighteenth century sees the invention of the Fashion Plate and the rise of journals devoted almost exclusively to changes in feminine modes.

The world inaugurated by the industrial revolution remained outwardly a world of privilege and class distinctions, but in reality it was a world in which there were only two classes: the rich and the poor. The only real Hierarchy was one of wealth, and in a plutocratic world the Seduction Principle in feminine dress necessarily reigned supreme. Hence the marked acceleration in changes in fashion.

Among men, however, the idea of gentility prevented a frank admission of what gods were really reigning and no nineteenth century millionaire thought of displaying his fortune on his back as an Elizabethan would have done without hesitation. Instead he bought for his wife the most fashionable (i.e. the most recent) clothes and put around her neck and wrists symbols of his riches in the form of precious stones. It is amusing to note that in modern America the symbolic bracelets have almost as much ritual significance as the gold stripes round an admiral's sleeve. Apart from this the Hierarchical Principle in women's dress has become merely vestigial—so many stripes of ermine on a coronation robe and the like—and the emergence of the emancipated young woman with money of her own to spend has introduced an entirely new element. We lack a name for this emancipated young woman but she certainly dominates fashion in the world today. In her own eyes she is the upholder of the Utility Principle (all young women seem to be convinced that their clothes are practical as well as beautiful) but the Seduction Principle is her real spring of action. She is opposed to the Hierarchical Principle and therefore the Fashion she dictates tends to blur class distinction.

She has been more successful in doing this than the men of her own social grade. Often it is quite impossible to tell what class a girl belongs to—until she opens her mouth or is joined by her boy friend. The social distinctions in male dress, subtle and obscure as they are, are much more difficult to eliminate.

Women have been helped in this by the activities of the great popularizers of Fashion, the fashion magazines and the film producers. In former times, even such comparatively recent times as the Edwardian period, it was the idle rich who set the mode. They could do so because they had a parade ground or shop window in the park, or even in the unhurried streets of the West End. Now they have no parade ground, and the theatre which once provided some kind of a shop window for the launching of new fashion, has been completely overshadowed by the film.

That influence, however, would have been ineffective but for the manufacturers of mass-produced clothes, who now take great pains to follow the mode as closely and as quickly as possible. Fashion designers have helped by catering directly for the new and immense market open before them—the young women of no particular social class with enough money to buy pretty clothes if they are reasonably priced.

During the last generation there has been an increasing margin of spending power among the masses, particularly the younger age group. Even working boys spend more on their clothes than they used to; girls spend much more. And they are probably right to do so since so much depends on personal appearance, for the sake of job prestige, general social prestige and attracting a mate.

Increased industrialization has meant a vast increase in the proportion of clerical and distributing workers as against workers in heavy industry and agriculture. And in the factory of the mass-production, machine-minding type, it is possible to keep up a high standard of clothes and appearance even at work. Where special clothes are necessary these tend to become stereotyped into uniforms, with no effect upon the forms of ordinary dress.

Shortly after the First World War there was an enormous improve-ment in the production of synthetic materials, in particular of artificial silk stockings, and this has done much to improve the appearance of working girls and to minimize the distance between them and more moneyed classes. Indeed there is hardly any luxury which is not, today, available to women of all social grades *in some form*, except the luxury of the absolute novelty of the model gown. In other words the only advantage the rich woman has over her poorer sisters is a fortnight's start. Even elaborate hairdressing, which in the eighteenth century created a gulf between those who could afford it and those who couldn't, has now become almost within the reach of all. Make-up also has been vastly improved, and this weapon the emancipated young woman has not hesitated to borrow from her once formidable but now almost extinct rival, the *grande cocotte*.

That all this tends to promote marriage between members of different classes and so to the progressive decline of class distinction, is obvious; that there will ever be any excessively rich people again seems more than doubtful. So far as woman is concerned the democratization of Fashion is both a cause and an effect.

To sum up: women's clothes have today abandoned the Hier-archical Principle completely. They represent a fairly stable balance between the Seduction Principle and the Utility Principle. Men have not recovered any Seduction Principle in their dress, which represents the rear-guard action of the Hierarchical Principle against the growing advance of the Utility Principle. We may possibly see some interesting developments in the next few years.

Meanwhile it would be a mistake to suppose that the problem is finally settled or indeed that it ever will be. Marxian man (and woman) may wish to dress only according to the Utility Principle; but Freudian man (and woman) will continue to obey the Seduction Principle. It is perhaps doubtful that Adlerian (or Nietzschean) man has been wholly scotched and Adlerian man constructs new Hierarchies as the old and obsolete ones are abolished. The Three Principles (and with them costume used as a means of Social Aggression) may be expected to continue to operate even in the Brave New World.

HUMAN AGGRESSION IN ANTHROPOLOGICAL PERSPECTIVE

By

DEREK FREEMAN

Institute of Advanced Studies, Australian National University, Canberra, Australia

E. J. DILLON (1896), having described in an article in the *Contemporary Review* the savage destructiveness and the terrible cruelties that had accompanied the massacres of the Armenians of Anatolia during the last decade of the nineteenth century, remarked that these happenings revealed "unimagined strata of malignity in the human heart".

History since that time has provided us with much further evidence of man's destructiveness as, equally, to use the words of Sir Carleton Kemp Allen (1957), of "cruelty on a large and hideous scale", with "the cold-blooded infamy of 'genocide'" and "psychological torments of unprecedented ingenuity" added to all "the crude old physical horrors".

But also, during this same period, the "unimagined strata of malignity" on which Dillon remarked have, for the first time in human history, been systematically explored, and, in particular, by the science of psycho-analysis.

Psycho-analytic recognition of the nature of aggression was, however, but gradual. Thus, although Freud (1905) early recognized impulses of cruelty as arising from sources independent of sexuality, these sources were, at first, traced to the self-preservative instincts and, at this period of his researches, Freud (1909) would not accept the existence of "a special instinct of aggression". It was not, indeed, until after the structure of the human psyche had been systematically explored and much additional clinical and historical evidence sifted that Freud came to his final conclusion that "the tendency to aggression is an innate, independent, instinctual disposition in man". This conclusion, which has been confirmed by subsequent research, is now one of the basic postulates of psychoanalytic theory.

What I want to do, as best I can within the limited confines of this present paper, is to survey the historical and anthropological evidence on human aggression, and, in particular, the palaeo-anthropological discoveries of the last two decades which have led to new interpretations of human evolution and to conclusions directly relevant to those reached by Freud.

In recent years there has been much important experimental research on aggression, as summarized, for example, by J. P. Scott (1958). This work has significantly extended our knowledge; however, if we are to understand adequately the realities of human aggression it is imperative that we should also pay close regard to the facts of history, for here we find, in profusion, happenings never likely to be enacted in a laboratory, and these are the phenomena which, in our theories, we must try to comprehend and explain.

Lewis Richardson, in his book *Statistics of Deadly Quarrels* (1960), has amassed some of the historical evidence for the period 1820–1945. Richardson calculates (p. 153) that during these 126 years, 59,000,000 human beings were killed in wars, murderous attacks, and other deadly quarrels. This huge total (which is, almost certainly, an under-estimate) is one indication of the magnitude of the natural phenomenon with which we are dealing. However, to comprehend the nature of human aggression, we must go beyond statistics to details of behaviour.

Much aggressive behaviour, I should stress at this juncture, is under ego control; it may, for example, be a reaction to a threat to self-preservation. In such instances, as Waelder (1960) has pointed out, aggression is an accessory to ego activities; here, in other words, destruction and cruelty are not ends in themselves, but rather, incidental to the achievement of ego purposes.

"However", continues Waelder, "there are also destructive manifestations which, through their character or intensity, lie outside of this area; manifestations of aggression which cannot be seen as reactive to provocation because they are so vast in intensity or duration that it would be difficult to fit them into any scheme of stimulus and reaction. . . ."

Much of the evidence for such "essential destructiveness" or "primary aggression" comes from psycho-pathology. Thus, Waelder refers to the fact that "a psychotic may strike his head with an axe with full force, and . . . repeat the assault if he has the strength left to do so;" and to "the sudden outbursts of catatonics, reaching out without warning from what seemed to be a state of indifference, to a lightning attack. . . ." In disturbed behaviour of these kinds, which are frequently observed among psychotics, aggression is starkly manifest, and provides, in Federn's view, the real basis for the assumption of a destructive drive.

Comparable behaviour is also to be encountered in plentitude in the annals of crime; just as human cruelty is prominently displayed in the tortures, mutilations and other punishments of exceeding severity which were once a common feature of the judicial process, and which, in some countries, still persist (Vidal-Naquet, 1963).

L. O. Pike, in his *A History of Crime in England* (1873 and 1876), has given a meticulously documented account of one part of the human record in these matters.

Similarly, there is an abundance of pertinent evidence in the facts of political history. For example, T. A. Walker, in his *A History of the Law of Nations* (1899), presents a scholarly survey of the practices that marked warfare from "the earliest times to the Peace of Westphalia, 1648". These practices, with but rare exceptions, exhibit extremes of destructiveness and cruelty, and, indeed, the epochs surveyed abound with happenings that differ scarcely at all from the phenomena of psycho-pathology.

I cannot, in such a brief paper, give any kind of adequate survey of the historical facts, but some indication of their nature is conveyed in this typical excerpt from Walker's *History* (p. 124), referring to the Middle Ages: "When Basil II (1014) could blind fifteen thousand Bulgarians, leaving an eye to the leader of every hundred, it ceases to be matter of surprise that Saracen marauders should thirty years later be impaled by Byzantine officials, that the Greeks of Adramyttium in the time of Malek Shah (1106–16) should drown Turkish children in boiling water, that the Emperor Nicephorus (961) should cast from catapults into a Cretan city the heads of Saracens slain in the attempt to raise the seige, or that a crusading Prince of Antioch (1097) should cook human bodies on spits to earn for his men the terrifying reputation of cannibalism".

The years that have elapsed since the Peace of Westphalia have not been without progress; but the course of human history has continued to be marked by wars, revolutions, massacres, rebellions and riots which have been characterized by destructiveness and cruelty no less extreme than that of earlier epochs. I have appended to this paper references which contain details of some of these events; a further listing of sources may be found in Richardson's *Statistics of Deadly Quarrels* (1960).

Any scholar who is prepared to examine objectively the evidence of history will be led, I believe, to the same conclusion as that reached by Durbin and Bowlby (1938), that no group of animals is "more aggressive or ruthless in their aggression than the adult members of the human race".

Indeed, the extreme nature of human destructiveness and cruelty is one of the principal characteristics which marks off man, behaviourally, from other animals. This point has been cogently expressed by the biologist Adolf Portman: ". . . when terrible things, cruelties hardly conceivable, occur among men, many speak thoughtlessly of 'brutality', of bestialism, or a return to animal levels. . . . As if there were animals which inflict on their own kind what men can do to men. Just at this point the zoologist has to draw a clear line: these evil, horrible things are no animal survival that happened to be carried along in the imperceptible transition from animal to man; this evil belongs entirely on this side of the dividing line, it is purely human. . . ." (Waelder, p. 147).

At this juncture let me remark that, despite the ubiquity of human aggression, we lack anything resembling an adequate history of human cruelty and destructiveness. There is, for example, no kind of scientific compilation of the essential facts, nor, for that matter, has the phenomenology of the behaviour that actually occurs in the course of massacres and other outbreaks of mass violence been fully reported and analysed. The full realities are, indeed, of a kind that cannot be generally published, and those who observe them readily repress much of the horror they have experienced. Dillon, for example, in his account of the Armenian massacres, after giving details of cruelties and mutilations of a gross kind, adds that there were others which "cannot be described, nor even hinted at". Indeed, in accounts of aggressive behaviour one constantly encounters the epithets "unbelievable", "indescribably", "unimaginable". In my view, there is great need for dispassionate research into the phenomenology of the aggressive behaviour of the human animal, for until we have come to see its realities for what they are, we shall not achieve a scientific understanding of these realities nor be able to evolve ways of controlling them.

The history of the more primitive peoples confirms the conclusions I have reached for the partially civilized. Davie (1929), having surveyed the ethnographic evidence, came to the conclusion that "war plays a prominent part in the lives of most primitive peoples, and is usually a sanguinary affair". There are some peoples, it is true, among whom aggressive behaviour and war are relatively rare; such cases are, however, "quite exceptional" in the ethnographic record. Moreover, these cases are, in general, those of puny and technically backward groups living under the dominance of alien, powerful and overtly aggressive neighbouring societies. In other words, we are here dealing with special forms of submissive adaptation. In the intra-group existence of such submissive peoples, however, as Ginsberg (1934) has noted, "violence and the fear of violence are there, and fighting occurs, though it is obviously and necessarily on a small scale".

With these few exceptions, the ethnographic evidence shows warfare among primitive peoples to have been endemic and, on occasion, internecine. Among some of the most primitive populations, indeed, aggressive behaviour is so endemic, between groups, as to dominate all aspects of their existence. Such a people are the Willigiman-Wallalua, of the Baliem valley of western New Guinea, whose lives are "an unending round of death and revenge", and who have recently been studied, in their uncontrolled state, by an anthropological expedition from Harvard University. Here, I would suggest, we have revealed the essentials of the pristine state of man.

Primitive cultures also exhibit many bizarre expressions of human cruelty and aggression, in sacrificial rites, ceremonies of initiation, ritual mutilations, head-hunting and cannibalistic cults, and murderous societies (like those of the thugs of historical India or the "leopard men" of Africa). These diverse forms of symbolic behaviour are paralleled by the highly aggressive fantasies to be found in mythologies throughout the world, and in the frightful torments of the various hells of human religions. Here we are dealing with delusional beliefs which have become shared and traditional; it is certain, however, that they are all, finally, endopsychic in origin and, therefore, products of the human unconscious. The violent character of these fantasies, and the fact that they are so often acted-out in ritual behaviour, present graphic evidence of the dynamic nature of the aggressive drive in the human animal.

Comparable evidence (as psycho-analytic research has demonstrated) is to be found in the dreams, fantasies and play of children. Again, as anyone who cares to study the history of blood-sports or the productions of the film industry can establish, spectacles of violence are a predominant element in the entertainments popular among men. Indeed, field observation shows that expressions of pleasure are basically associated with the witnessing of destruction and the infliction of hurt—the most common of these expressions being that of involuntary and cathected laughter.

William James (1911), in discussing "the rooted bellicosity of human nature", described man as "biologically considered . . . the most formidable of all the beasts of prey, and indeed, the only one that preys systematically on its own species". Here, James was pointing to one of the forms of behaviour, that of cannibalism, by which the human animal may be sharply distinguished from other primates. Cannibalism, which is but one expression of man's carnivorous nature, has been reported for almost all parts of the world, and, on the evidence of palaeo-anthropology, was probably once a universal practice. Blanc (1961) has shown that a range of fossil skulls, from the mid-Pleistocene onwards, are characterized by a "careful and symmetric incising of the periphery of the *foramen magnum*" to produce an opening which, on comparative evidence, was made with the purpose of extracting the brain for eating. Blanc also remarks that ritual theophagy (such as that of ancient Greece in which a goat, symbolizing Dionysus, was eaten), obviously had its origin in former ritual cannibalism, and notes that St. Paul, in his Letter to the Corinthians stresses with particular strength "the real presence of Christ's blood and flesh in the Eucharistic ritual", this being "a powerful means of promoting the penetration and acceptance of Christianity and its major ritual in Greece where the tradition of the Dionysiac symbolic ritual meal was particularly strong and deeply felt". As a codicil to this commentary on the origin of theophagy and its deep appeal to the human animal, let me direct attention to the age-old association of fanaticism and aggression, and record that in sixteenth century England, denial of the real presence was one of the offences for which heretics were punished, under statute, by being publicly burnt alive (Pike, 1876). Indeed, human aggression is never more terrifying than when at the service of the dogmatic and delusory group ideologies characteristic of *Homo sapiens*: "When truth kills truth, O devilish-holy fray!" So (Durbin and Bowlby, 1938) will men "die like flies for theories and exterminate each other with every instrument of destruction for abstractions".

I have now sketched, in very summary fashion, some of the principal manifestations of human aggression. In the past these basic aspects of human behaviour have been attributed (as by Rousseau, Eliot Smith and others) to the state of civilization, it being argued that man was "a being naturally good", and that the "earliest forms of man must have been, in the main, harmless, frugivorous animals" (Eisler, 1951).

The time when such views might be entertained by informed scholars is now, however, past, for the discoveries of palaeo-anthropology during the past two decades have, in fundamental ways, transformed our comprehension of the origin of man and of the probable processes of human evolution.

Darwin, in 1871, expressed the view that it was "somewhat more probable that our early progenitors lived on the African continent than elsewhere"; this speculation has, during the present century, been borne out by the discovery of such fossil primate forms as *Propliopithecus* (of the Oligocene of Egypt), *Proconsul* and *Limno-pithecus* (of the Miocene of Kenya) and of the lower Pleistocene hominids of eastern and southern Africa, which I shall refer to collectively as the Australopithecinae.

The first Australopithecine fossil, *Australopithecus africanus*, was discovered at Taungs, in Bechuanaland, in 1924, and described by Raymond Dart. Since then additional major discoveries have been made by Broom, Robinson and Dart in South Africa, and by Leakey (in 1959) at the Olduvai Gorge, Tanganyika (of *Zinjan-thropus boisei*, the skull and other bones of which were found on the living floor of an ancient camping site in association with stone tools, a hammer stone and flakes).

The limb and pelvic bones of the Australopithecinae indicate that these hominids walked erect. This is an important fact, for, as Darwin and others have stressed, the attainment of bipedal locomotion is a crucial stage in the transition from ape to man, for by freeing the hands it makes possible the evolution of the employment and manufacture of weapons and tools. A concomitant process in this evolutionary development is a reduction in the size of the teeth and of the facial skeleton. This condition we also find in the Australo-pithecinae, whose teeth are small and of human conformation. Furthermore, the Australopithecinae were typically found (Bartho-lomew and Birdsell, 1953) in association with the mammalian fauna of the open grasslands of southern Africa, on which fauna they carnivorously preyed.

The evidence for the carnivorous adaptation of the Australopithecinae, and of their employment of lethal weapons (despite the relative smallness of their brains, which were in the range 450–600 c.c.), was first summarily stated by Raymond Dart in 1953, in his paper *The Predatory Transition from Ape to Man*; and this was followed, in 1957, by the detailed publication by the Transvaal Museum of the archaeological data on which Dart's views were based, in his monograph *The Osteodontokeratic Culture of Australopithecus Prometheus*, in which the weapons of bone, tooth and horn employed by these hominids of the lower Pleistocene are fully described, illustrated and discussed, as are their predatory, murderous and cannibalistic predilictions.

The Australopithecinae, then, are an evolutionary innovation, a primate species that, becoming terrestrial, achieved an unprecedented evolutionary advance by a predatory and carnivorous adaptation to their new environment, based on an upright stance and the adoption of lethal, manual weapons.

We are here confronted with events of great consequence for the understanding of man's nature, and of his emergence as a dominant species on this planet.

The predatory adaptation achieved by the Australopithecinae involved, we may infer, "a behavioural transition from a retreating to an attacking pattern" (Freedman and Roe, 1958), and to related changes of a phylogenetic kind. Prehistoric man was a hunter, and may be distinguished from all other living primates by his predatory habits which are well established by the Pithecanthropine evidence as well as that for the rest of the Palaeolithic period. With the discovery of the Australopithecinae and the nature of their highly specialized cultural adaptation to a predatory way of life, the palaeo-anthropological evidence presents a prospect of human evolution in which, possibly since the lower Pleistocene, "carnivorous curiosity and aggression have been added to the inquisitiveness and dominance striving of the ape" (Washburn and Avis, 1958).

"Man", Washburn (1959) has recently written, "has a carnivorous psychology. It is easy to teach people to kill, and it is hard to develop customs which avoid killing. Many human beings enjoy seeing other human beings suffer, or enjoy the killing of animals ... public beatings and tortures are common in many cultures."

These human characteristics are seen, in the light of the recent discoveries of palaeo-anthropology, to be phylogenetic: the pervasive aggression and cruelty of historic man, by which he is differentiated from other primates, is explicable, to use the words of Raymond Dart (1953) "only in terms of his carnivorous and cannibalistic origins".

It is significant, I would remark, that palaeo-anthropology has, during the last decade, revealed a phylogenetic basis for the conculsions about human aggression which have been reached by psycho-analytic research into man's nature. The view taken by these two sciences is, furthermore, substantiated by general historical and ethnographical evidence.

I cannot here hope to survey all of the implications for evolutionary theory of the Australopithecine evidence, but I would like to indicate very briefly one or two of the more important of them. The Australopithecinae, we have seen, were hominids with small brains (in the range 450–600 c.c.) who, nonetheless, used manual implements. The principal inferences to be drawn from these facts (Washburn, 1959) are that the evolution of the highly competent human hand occurred as a result of the new selective pressures that were initiated by the adoption of weapons and tools, and that the real increase in the brain size of the human species, of approximately three times, which took place during the Pleistocene, was also the result of this new cultural adaptation.

Confirmatory evidence for this hypothesis is to be found in the researches of Penfield and his associates (1952, 1959) on the localization of function in the cerebral cortex of man. In the monkey motor cortex (Woolsey and Settlage, 1950) the area associated with the hand is approximately as large as that for the foot. In the human brain, however, the area for the hand is relatively much larger. This, as Washburn (1959) has noted, supports the view that "the increase in the size of the brain occurred after the use of tools, and that selection for more skilful tool-using resulted in changes in the proportions of the hand, and of the parts of the hand (including primary motor and sense areas, and the areas concerned with the elaboration of skills)".

In broad anthropological perspective then, it may be argued that man's nature and skills and, ultimately, human civilization, owe their existence to the kind of predatory adaptation first achieved by the carnivorous Australopithecinae on the grasslands of southern Africa in the lower Pleistocene.

At the present stage of progress of human civilization, however, the aggressive disposition which served evolutionary development at various times in the past is perhaps man's most basic and difficult problem. It is not my purpose in this paper to discuss the methods by which human aggression may be controlled; let me merely, on this present occasion, state again my conviction that it is only by facing the realities of man's nature and of our extraordinary history as a genus that we shall be able to evolve methods likely, in some measure, to succeed.

References

Alexander, F. 1941. "The Psychiatric Aspects of War and Peace." *American Journal of Sociology*, **46**, 504-520.
Allen, C. K. 1958. *Aspects of Justice.* London: Stevens and Sons.
Anon. 1896. "The Constantinople Massacre". *Contemporary Review*, **70**, 457-465.

Ardrey, R. 1961. *African Genesis*. London: Collins.
Astor, D. 1962. "Towards a Study of the Scourge". *Encounter*, August.
Bartholomew, G. A., and Birdsell, J. B. 1953. "Ecology and the Proto-hominids". *American Anthropologist*, **55**, 481-498.
Blanc, A. C. 1961. "Some Evidence for the Ideologies of Early Man," in *Social Life of Early Man*. Edited by S. L. Washburn. Chicago: Viking Fund Publications in Anthropology No. 31.
Broom, R., and Schepers, G. W. H. 1946. *The South African Fossil Ape-Men, the Australopithecinae*. Pretoria: Transvaal Museum Memoir No. 2.
Clark, W. E. Le Gros. 1958. *History of the Primates: An Introduction to the Study of Fossil Man*. 6th Edition. London: British Museum (Natural History).
Corfield, F. D. 1960. *Historical Survey of the Origins and Growth of Mau Mau*. London: Her Majesty's Stationery Office.
Darwin, C. 1871. *The Descent of Man*. New York: Modern Library Edition (1949).
Dart, R. 1925. "*Australopithecus africanus:* The Man-ape of South Africa." *Nature*, **115**, 195-199.
Dart, R. 1953. "The Predatory Transition from Ape to Man." *International Anthropological and Linguistic Review*, **1**, 201-219.
Dart, R. 1957. *The Osteodontokeratic Culture of Australopithecus Prometheus*. Pretoria: Transvaal Museum Memoir No. 10.
Dart, R. 1959. *Adventures with the Missing Link*. New York: Harper and Brothers.
Davie, M. R. 1929. *The Evolution of War*. New Haven: Yale University Press.
Dillon, E. J. 1896. "Armenia: An Appeal." *Contemporary Review*, **69**, 1-19.
Dollard, J., Doob, L. W., Miller, N. E., Mowrer, O. H., and Sears, R. R. 1939. *Frustration and Aggression*. New Haven: Yale University Press.
Durbin, E. F. M., and Bowlby, J. 1938. "Personal Aggressiveness and War," in *War and Democracy: Essays on the Causes and Prevention of War*. Edited by E. F. M. Durbin and George Catlin. London: Kegan Paul.
East, W. N. 1948. "Sexual Crime". *The Journal of Criminal Science*, **1**, 45-83.
Eisler, R. 1951. *Man into Wolf*. London: Routledge and Kegan Paul.
Federn, P. 1952. *Ego Psychology and the Psychoses*. New York: Basic Books.
Freedman, L. Z., and Roe, A. 1958. "Evolution and Human Behaviour," in *Behaviour and Evolution*. Edited by A. Roe and G. G. Simpson. New Haven: Yale University Press.
Freud, Anna 1953. "The Bearing of the Psychoanalytic Theory of Instinctual Drives on Certain Aspects of Human Behaviour," in *Drives, Affects, Behaviour*. Edited by Rudolph M. Loewenstein. New York: International Universities Press.
Freud, Sigmund 1905. *Three Essays on the Theory of Sexuality*. Standard Edition, Vol. VII. London: Hogarth Press.
Freud, Sigmund 1909. *Analysis of a Phobia in a Five-Year-Old Boy*. Standard Edition, Vol. X. London: Hogarth Press.
Freud, Sigmund 1930. *Civilization and its Discontents*. Standard Edition, Vol. XXI. London: Hogarth Press.
Freud, Sigmund 1932. *Why War?* Collected Papers, Vol. V. London: Hogarth Press.
Ginsberg, M., and Glover, E. 1934. "A Symposium on the Psychology of Peace and War." *The British Journal of Medical Psychology*, **14**, 274-293.
Glover, E. 1946. *War, Sadism and Pacifism*. London: George Allen and Unwin.
Goya. 1808. *Desastres de la Guerra*, in *Goya: Complete Etchings, Aquatints and Lithographs*. Edited by E. L. Ferrari. London: Thames and Hudson (1962).
Hartmann, H., Kris, E., and Lowenstein, R. M. 1950. "Notes on the Theory of Aggression," *The Psycho-Analytic Study of the Child*, **3-4**, 9-36.
Hogg, G. 1958. *Cannibalism and Human Sacrifice*. London: Robert Hale.
James, W. 1911. *Memories and Studies*. London: Longmans, Green and Co. P. 301.

Klein, Melanie 1949. *The Psycho-Analysis of Children.* London: Hogarth Press.
Kroeber, A. L. 1928. "Sub-Human Culture Beginnings." *The Quarterly Review of Biology,* **3**, 325-342.
Langer, W. L. 1951. *The Diplomacy of Imperialism,* 1890-1902. New York: Knopf.
Leaky, L. S. B. 1960. "The Origin of the Genus Homo," in *The Evolution of Man.* Edited by Sol Tax. Chicago: University of Chicago Press.
Le Bon, G. 1913. *The Psychology of Revolution.* London: Fisher Unwin.
Lissagaray. 1898. *History of the Commune of* 1871. New York: International Publishing Co.
McClintock, F. H., and Gibson, Evelyn. 1961. *Robbery in London.* London: Macmillan.
Menninger, K. 1938. *Man Against Himself.* New York: Harcourt, Brace and Co.
Moon, P. 1962. *Divide and Quit.* London: Chatto and Windus.
Montagu, M. F. Ashley. 1960. *An Introduction to Physical Anthropology.* 3rd Edition. Springfield: Charles C. Thomas.
Oakley, K. 1957. "Tools Makyth Man." *Antiquity,* **31**, 199-209.
Pelham, C. 1887. *The Chronicles of Crime, or The New Newgate Calendar.* 2 vols. London: T. Miles and Co.
Penfield, W., and Rasmussen, T. 1952. *The Cerebral Cortex of Man: A Clinical Study of Localization of Function.* New York: Macmillan.
Penfield, W., and Roberts, L. 1959. *Speech and Brain Mechanism.* Princeton: Princeton University Press.
Phillips, R. 1949. *Trial of Josef Kramer and Forty-four Others* (The Belsen Trial). London: William Hodge and Co.
Pike, L. O. 1873 and 1876. *A History of Crime in England.* 2 Vols. London: Smith, Elder and Co.
Portman, A. 1942. *Grenzen des Lebens.* Basel: Friederich Reinhardt.
Redl, F., and Wineman, D. 1957. *The Aggressive Child.* Glencoe: Free Press.
Reel, A. F. 1949. *The Case of General Yamashita.* Chicago: University of Chicago Press.
Richardson, L. F. 1960. *Statistics of Deadly Quarrels.* London: Stevens and Sons.
Rifkin, A. H. 1963. "Violence in Human Behaviour" (Report on Symposium at the A.A.A.S. meeting, December, 1962). *Science,* **40**, 904-906.
Russell, Lord (of Liverpool). 1954. *The Scourge of the Swastika.* London: Cassell.
Schilder, P. 1951. *Psychoanalysis, Man and Society.* New York: Norton.
Scott, J. P. 1958. *Aggression.* Chicago: University of Chicago Press.
Sears, Pauline S. 1951. "Doll Play Aggression in Normal Young Children: Influence of Sex, Age, Sibling Status, Father's Absence." *Psychological Monographs,* **65** (6), 1-42.
Sleeman, C., and Silkin, S. C. 1951. *Trial of Sumida Haruzo and Twenty Others* (The *"Double Tenth"* Trial). London: William Hodge.
Sleeman, W. H. 1836. *Ramaseena.* Calcutta: Military Orphan Press.
Stekel, W. 1953. *Sadism and Masochism: The Psychology of Hatred and Cruelty.* 2 Vols. New York: Liveright.
Strachey, A. 1957. *The Unconscious Motives of War.* London: Allen and Unwin.
Taylor, M. 1839. *Confessions of a Thug.* London: O.U.P. (World Classics, 1916).
Thrasher, F. M. 1936. *The Gang.* Chicago: University of Chicago Press.
Tuker, F. 1950. *While Memory Serves.* London: Cassell.
Turberville, A. S. 1949. *The Spanish Inquisition.* London: O.U.P.
Vidal-Naquet, P. 1963. *Torture: Cancer of Democracy, France and Algeria,* 1954-62. London: Penguin Books.
Von Bertalanffy, L. 1958. "Comments on Aggression." *Bulletin of the Menninger Clinic,* **22**, 50-57.

Waelder, R. 1960. *Basic Theory of Psychoanalysis.* New York: International Universities Press. Pp. 141-142.

Walker, T. A. 1899. *A History of the Law of Nations. Vol. I: From the Earliest Times to the Peace of Westphalia,* 1648. Cambridge: C.U.P.

Washburn, S. L., and Avis, V. 1958. "Evolution of Human Behaviour," in *Behaviour and Evolution.* Edited by A. Roe and G. G. Simpson. New Haven: Yale University Press.

Washburn, S. L. 1959. "Speculations on the Inter-relations of the History of Tools and Biological Evolution," in *The Evolution of Man's Capacity for Culture.* Edited by J. N. Spuhler. Detroit: Wayne State University Press.

Washburn, S. L., and Howell, F. C. 1960. "Human Evolution and Culture," in *The Evolution of Man.* Edited by Sol Tax. Chicago: University of Chicago Press.

Washburn, S. L., and De Vore, I. 1961. "Social Behaviour of Baboons and Early Men," in *Social Life of Early Men.* Edited by S. L. Washburn. Chicago: Viking Fund Publications in Anthropology, No. 31.

Whitman, H. 1951. *Terror in the Streets.* New York: Dial Press.

Woolsey, C. N., and Settlage, P. H. 1950. "Pattern of Localization in the Precentral Cortex of *Macaca Mulatta.*" *Fed. Proc. Amer. Soc. Exp. Biol.,* 9, 140.

Wright, Q. 1942. *A Study of War.* 2 Vols. Chicago: University of Chicago Press.

Zuckerman, S. 1932. *The Social Life of Monkeys and Apes.* London: Kegan Paul.

HARRISON: I have noticed in this and in other papers of a psychological nature, reprints of which have been circularized for this symposium, that there appears to be a divergence of views between psychologists and biologists in the interpretation of the differing kinds of behaviour. As a biologist I can recognize in a variety of organisms, when individuals come together, on the one hand an attacking drive, or aggressive drive, or action; and on the other a fleeing drive, a submissive drive, or a reaction. These appear to be opposing tendencies. A sex drive may be present as a third component creating a tendency for the two individuals to remain together, and giving rise to conflicts between both the attacking and the fleeing drive and the sex drive. It seems to me that the psychologists have recognized the existence of the aggressive drive, but appear to regard as its opposite what they describe by the rather loose terms of "love" and "affection". They appear to have lumped both fleeing and sex drives, and conflict of sex drives with either attacking or fleeing, under the latter heading, without discriminating between them, and this would appear to have led to some confusion in the interpretation of aggressive behaviour and the responses to it.

LORENZ: I think we have, in the course of this discussion imperceptively widened the conception of what we call aggression. I think we ought to come back to the functional definition of intraspecific aggression as attempted by Dr. Storr and myself in our presentations.

STORR: Professor Hill stated that aggressive manifestations against self increased with age, but this is not true of all aggressive behaviour. Does he not consider that nail-biting and hair-pulling which are much commoner in children, are also aggressive manifestations directed against the self and decrease with age?

HILL: It is true that minor self-mutilations are commoner in children than in adults, but it must be remembered that excoriation of the skin and picking are very common again in the senium. Nevertheless the serious forms of aggression turned upon the self-depressive illness and successful suicide, are increasingly common as age advances.

LORENZ: Constant stimulation of aggression, as for instance frustration, may help to keep fighting fit. One of my pupils, Walter Heiligenberg, has recently shown quantitatively that constant activation is necessary to keep aggressive behaviour "in training". In other words, it is subject to atrophy if kept inactive too long. This, however, does not change the fact that drives are endogenously generated and that energy is needed to repress them. The chief and, in my opinion, most important point of agreement between psycho-analysis and ethology concerns this dynamic side of instinct physiology.

HARRISON: Does Professor Hill consider that suicide is always a form of aggressive behaviour and never a form of escape?

HILL: Yes, I think that suicide, successful or unsuccessful, is always a form of aggressive behaviour but it may also be interpreted on many occasions as a form of escape as well.

HARRISON: I have enjoyed Mr. Laver's paper but would like to question the "Seduction Principle". I would suggest that women do not dress to attract the opposite sex but to be "one up" on other women. (In any case sexual recognition would appear to function quite irrespective of clothing.) Fashion would appear to have a function in establishing for an individual a position of dominance within a large subordinate group which is competing for the attention of a smaller dominant group. There has been an unusual opportunity for studying this in recent years in adolescent groups where the earlier sex ratio has been reversed and there are now more boys than girls. At the same time that this change has occurred there has been a change in behaviour, the boys showing a tendency to attach great importance to elaborate dress and also to show other characters of behaviour which were earlier regarded as feminine. Also at the same time there has been an increasing casualness and relaxation in the standard of dress shown by the girls. I have had the opportunity to observe groups of such boys and I have found that the clothes were worn, not to attract girls, but to establish a position of superiority and dominance within the group. This would, of course, indirectly give a selective advantage in attracting sexual recognition. In such circumstances we may suspect that the importance of fashion will depend on the relative position of the two sexes as regards numbers, and not be peculiar to one of them.

LAVER: The motive of women in dressing has always caused controversy. Most women indignantly deny that they dress to attract the opposite sex. They dress, they say, to please themselves. I have, however, devised a formula which I hope will make everybody happy: "Women dress in competition with other women, to please themselves by attracting men". The idea of dominance within a group (e.g. gangs of teenagers) only operates in semi-barbaric societies. The "gentleman" merely wishes to indicate his membership of a class. He would repudiate the idea of distinguishing him, inside it, by his dress. I do not think that the ratio of the sexes is the dominant factor except in such groups. The erotic factor (the Seduction Principle) as applied to male dress is conspicuously absent elsewhere.

OAKLEY: Would Mr. Laver apply the same or a similar classification to night-clothes as to day-clothes? (He explained that he meant night-dresses and the like, sleeping-clothes!) Was it not true that these were unknown in Britain before about 1800, coming into use at about the same time as wall-paper? Would he agree that the fashions in "sleeping-clothes" might serve as an index of social changes during the last century or two?

LAVER: Night-clothes are a specialized study. As Mr. Oakley says, they were almost unknown before about 1800. In the Middle Ages both sexes slept naked. Later the men wore their day shirts, the women their shifts. I do not understand the relevance of the reference to wallpaper. Wall-paper, in a rather primitive form, is known in the sixteenth century. Pyjamas are largely twentieth century, but only men of the upper classes wore them until 1914. In the First World War they were provided for officers only. Women began to wear them in the '20s. Women have recently gone back to nightdresses, some of them of the extremely short "baby doll" variety.

CARTHY: I wonder whether the development of weapons used at a distance might increase aggression by putting space between the two men so that gestures of submission became ineffective. What evidence is there of the use by the Australopithecinae of weapons which were thrown? I believe it has been suggested that they threw stones at baboons.

FREEMAN: Dr. Carthy's suggestion is, I think, of great interest. There is good ethological evidence that in many species gestures of submission do tend to inhibit aggression, and the invention of weapons capable of being used at a distance (which has been a constant trend in the evolution of weapons) is certainly counter to any such natural inhibitory process.

Here is a problem which might well be taken up by ethologists and anthropologists alike. Stones thrown from the hand are used most effectively by primitive peoples, both in hunting and in war; of the early Hottentots, for example, it is said they used "showers of stones" in war, and that "the most amazing strokes of Hottentot dexterity are seen in their throwing of a stone" (Clark, 1959). Kortlandt and Kooij (1963) have recently surveyed agonistic throwing among infra-human primates. On this, and other evidence, I would suppose that early hominids, like the Australopithecinae, were capable of such throwing. One of the postcards on sale at the British Museum (Natural History), I recollect, shows Australopithicus rushing forward, threatening, with a stone in his upraised hand. Dart (1957) has argued that some of the long bones found at Australopithecine sites were used as clubs, and almost certainly produced the matching, indented fractures seen on associated baboon skulls. It is not unlikely that stones were also used.

HUXLEY: It seems probable that a decisive step in recurring hominid dominance was the use of weapons (clubs and especially spears), both for predation and for defence against predators and especially rivals.

FREEMAN: Yes, I would agree on the decisive importance of weapons, but these included many types in addition to clubs and spears.

HUXLEY: Spears and clubs, being wooden, would not survive whereas the (non-aggressive) pebble tools characteristic of the Australopithecinae would.

FREEMAN: It is true that wooden weapons would not survive, but incorrect that pebble tools were characteristic of the Australopithecinae (Clark, 1959). The evidence amassed by Dart (1957) indicates that the weapons of the Australopithecinae were of bone, teeth and horn, and that these weapons represent an evolutionary stage antecedent to the working of pebbles. It is likely that rudimentary wooden clubs (i.e. branches, etc.) were also used. Kortlandt and Kooij (1963) have recently discussed agonistic clubbing by chimpanzees.

LORENZ: Animals can be made to behave like men and massacre the fellow-members of their own species. If one crowds a dozen roe deer into a pen in a zoo, the most gory massacre is the result. I think that Professor Washburn in the sentence quoted by Dr. Freeman ("Man has a carnivorous psychology") does grave injustice to carnivores. Those that have power to hurt most grievously by using their hunting weapons usually have correspondingly reliable inhibiting mechanisms preventing them from hurting the fellow-members of their species. Wolves and lions do not usually commit massacre even under abnormally crowded conditions.

FREEMAN: I fully accept what Professor Lorenz has said in defence of lions, wolves and other carnivores. It is not possible for me to answer for Professor Washburn, whose words I have quoted, but I am sure he would, with me, deplore injustice being done to such noble creatures. My own view is that the term carnivorous when it is used to refer to the behaviour of the Hominidae has to give a meaning quite distinct from that which it has when applied to species within the order Carnivora.

HUXLEY: Carnivorous predators are not aggressive in the customary sense when hunting—only when attacked. Herbivores like rhino, African buffalo and elephant are among the most aggressive of animals. There is no correlation between diet and aggressivity.

FREEMAN: Sir Julian Huxley's statements about the carnivores and herbivores known to zoology, I accept, but I would question whether such findings can be automatically applied to the human animal. A snare here is the term carnivorous, which would seem to have a somewhat different meaning for zoologist and anthropologist. For the zoologist it is an epithet he applies to any carnivore. Literally carnivorous means "feeding on flesh", and it is, therefore, a fitting word to describe such feeding by the human animal. Feeding on flesh was a major feature of hominid adaptation during the one or two million years of the Pleistocene, and (in most cultures) it remains the habit of contemporary man, with the innovation that today it is the flesh of domesticated rather than hunted animals on which men feed. However, when as an anthropologist I refer to the Hominidae as being carnivorous I am certainly not classing them with members of the order Carnivora. On present evidence the carnivorous habit characteristic of the Hominidae emerged, during the Pleistocene, with the evolution of manual weapons and an adaptation based on hunting. It is possible, however, that a predilection for flesh-eating and a capacity to capture some kinds of prey may have been in existence before the evolution of actual weapons; and these developments, indeed, may have been among the selective pressures which led to the devising of rudimentary manual weapons by the Australopithecinae, and early members of the genus Homo, such as (possibly) *Homo habilis* (Leakey, Tobias and Napier, 1964). Evidence for this hypothesis is to be found in the recently published researches of Miss Jane Goodall (of Newnham College, Cambridge) on the behaviour of wild chimpanzees (*Pan satyrus schweinfurthi*) in Tanganyika. Miss Goodall reports having observed the capture, killing and eating of a red colobus monkey by one of these wild chimpanzees (Goodall, 1963a), and, on other occasions, the eating of "a very young bushpig", and "a bushbuck about one month old" (Goodall, 1963b). The predatory adaptations of hominids during the Pleistocene were plainly of a markedly different kind from those which have evolved, by phylogenetically distinct processes, among the Carnivora. Further, in the case of the hominids, we may possibly be dealing with animals which evolved lethal manual weapons and became predatory and carnivorous, but who lacked the efficacious, phylogenetically given inhibitory mechanisms of the Carnivora. So, in the light of recent palaeo-anthropological discoveries, the hypothesis has now been advanced that certain aspects of human nature (including possibly aggressivity and cruelty) may well be connected with the special predatory and carnivorous adaptations which were so basic to hominid evolution during the Pleistocene period. This, in my view, is an hypothesis that deserves to be investigated scientifically and dispassionately, for it concerns matters about which we are, at present, most ignorant.

CHANCE: It has been found by Dr. Oxnard that many monkeys imported into this country become deficient in vitamin B12, because they are no longer fed on animal food; hence there may be an association between the animal protein requirements of primates and their hunting habits, if what is true of the macaque can also be said of man. Which came first, the vitamin requirement or the hunting, we may never find out.

KALMUS: You stated in your lecture that about four times as many men commit suicide than women, and that the maximum incidence is at the age of about 70 years. In an aside during the discussion you then described as typical for an unsuccessful suicide attempt "the errant male partner anxiously waiting at the bed of the recovering female". This to my mind implies that the sex incidence, age distribution and possibly motivation of successful suicide and attempted suicide are quite different. Would you agree with these conclusions and would you say a few words concerning the differences in motivation?

HILL: Yes, I would agree in general with what you have said. One must clearly distinguish between the majority of successful and the majority of unsuccessful suicides, while the former occurs most frequently in older people, the latter are commoner in the young adults and there is probably not the same sex difference. The suicidal attempt is often clearly motivated—not to achieve self-destruction but to achieve revenge or to manipulate an unhappy social situation. Many people who make suicidal gestures do so in a state of great anger and frustration and sometimes, of course, they go too far.

HARRISON: Dr. Freeman has suggested that at a certain period in evolution man became much more aggressive in his behaviour. This would seem to have occurred at the time when men were tending to group themselves in larger units and there must have been a need to inhibit aggressive behaviour within the group together with a need for an outlet for such damned-up aggression. This aggression might then be canalized and an individual outside the group might be the recipient of the redirected aggression of the entire group. In such circumstances there might not be an increase in the amount of aggressive behaviour present in man but a great manifestation of it when it was redirected by an entire group to a single end.

FREEMAN: I would agree that Dr. Harrison has drawn attention to a basic process in the aggressive behaviour between tribes and nations which has characterized human history. It is also a process, I would add, very much to be found within societies. There is, for example, often considerable inhibition of aggression under parental dominance within the family, and this may lead to the redirection of aggressive impulses within the family, as also on to others beyond the family, but within the same society. The whole question of the redirection of aggression within and by human groups is, I consider, eminently worthy of intensive further study.

CARTHY: As ethologists we are used to seeing a decoration of an animal and finding that it is flaunted in display. Does Mr. Laver think that the same principle applies with the ruff, or lace cuffs, for example, in domestic dress as opposed to military costume?

LAVER: Certainly the ruff was a kind of display, a flaunting, and the connection between it and similar animal decorations would repay study. The lace ruffle at the wrist obviously lent itself to flaunting gestures. I don't think there is any distinction here between civil and military dress.

LORENZ: Professor Otto Koenig in Vienna has recently made a study of military uniforms and their relationship to human threat attitudes, and found many interesting correlations.

OAKLEY: Dr. Derek Freeman has referred to the "Osteodontokeratic culture" of the Australopithecines as evidence of the aggressiveness of the earliest hominids. As I have had the opportunity to examine the evidence I feel that in this field we must separate fact from inference and speculation. I have great admiration for Professor Raymond Dart's contribution to palaeo-anthropology in discovering *Australopithecus* and above all for recognizing its hominid status, which was so hotly denied until recently by many distinguished anatomists. However, I was one of the slow ones in being convinced that the antelope bone piles at Makapansgat and the fractured baboon skulls at Taung represented the predatory habits of *Australopithecus*. There is no longer any doubt in my mind that the earliest hominids had become meat-eaters. The Makapansgat evidence could be interpreted as indicating that as regards the larger mammals these early hominids were largely scavangers, i.e. meat-collectors rather than hunters, for which they were ill-equipped; but the evidence from the "living-floor" of *Zinjanthropus*, the East African australopithecine, shows that this hominid was killing small animals and the young of larger mammals. He was becoming a hunter, regularly adding meat to his diet.

The South African australopithecines no doubt developed the same dietary habits or they would not have survived on the dry veldt; but I think it is going beyond legitimate inference to interpret the broken "meat-bones" as daggers and saws. The bones were broken to extract marrow; about one per cent of the bones in the Makapansgat midden shows signs of *use*, but that is a different matter from inferring that any of them were made into killing tools (weapons). As Sir Julian Huxley has pointed out, if a hominid regularly kills other animals as food this does not necessarily imply that he was aggressive or a killer of other men. One of the australopithecine arm-bones from Makapansgat has been used as a scoop, but inference from this should remain open. There is no doubt that *Pithecanthropus* of the Pekin Caves half a million years ago ate the brains of his fellow men; but, as one of the speakers said, these may have been men of the same species yet of neighbouring groups How can we tell? Even at this early time level must we rule out the possibility of ritualized behaviour? The earliest use of what were probably missile-stones was not long after the beginning of hunting, perhaps a million years ago or more. The oldest evidence of the use of wooden spears is from deposits of the Second Interglacial age (? quarter of a million years ago). There was no organized warfare before the Neolithic period, beginning less than 10,000 years ago.

HUXLEY: I have recently seen an extraordinary film made by Osmond, Hoffer and Fogd, which showed drastic personality changes produced by hypnotically induced changes in perception Thus a suggested brightness of all colours tended to a hypnomanic state, with rather aggressive behaviour, while suggested inability to perceive any colour produced a depressive state. The most remarkable effects were produced by altering the time-sense. When this was too much speeded up, the subject became violently aggressive and truly manic. When "time was made to stop" (by stopping the metronome which the subject had been told would beat at the rate of one per second), the subject became catatonic with Waxy-flexibility.

Further experiments have shown that when two persons are put together who have received the suggestion that they would see everything in the same colour (e.g. blue), they tend to be amicable; whereas when two persons are put together who have received the suggestion that they would see everything in different colours (e.g. one in blue, the other in red), they tend to quarrel and to become aggressive towards each other.

References

Clark, J. Desmond. 1959. *The Pre-history of Southern Africa.* Penguin: Harmonsworth.

Goodall, Jane. 1963a. "My Life Among Wild Chimpanzees." *National Geographic Magazine*, **124**, 272-308.

Goodall, Jane. 1963b. "Feeding Behaviour of Wild Chimpanzees." *Symposium No. 10, The Zoological Society of London*, 39-48.

Kortlandt, A., and Kooij, M. 1963. "Protohominid Behaviour in Primates." *Symposium No. 10, The Zoological Society of London*, 61-88.

Krohn, P. L., Oxnard, C. E., and Chalmers, J. N. M. 1963. "Vitamin B12 in the Serum of the Rhesus Monkey." *Nature*, **197**, 186.

Leakey, L. S. B., Tobias, P. V., and Napier, J. R. 1964. "A New Species of the Genus Homo from Olduvai Gorge." *Nature*, Vol. 202, No. 4927, 7-9.

Oxnard, C. E. 1964. "Some Variations in the Amount of Vitamin B12 in the Serum of the Rhesus Monkey." *Nature*, **201**, 1188-1191.

ORIGINS OF WAR

By

STANISLAV ANDRESKI

Department of Sociology, University of Reading, England

ALL types of human activity must have emerged at some point of time, but whereas some of them (like science or machine industry) came into existence in the full light of historical records, the origins of others are enveloped in eternal obscurity. The origins of capitalism or even the art of writing constitute a subject for argument based on evidence, but only tenuous conjectures can be offered on the problem of the origins of language, religion or war.

The question of the origins of war is even more hopeless than that of the origins of the state, because we know a great deal about primitive groups and tribes which are stateless in the sense of being without anything that can be called a government. Moreover, there are historical records describing a number of cases of emergence of a state.* Nothing comparable exists as far as war is concerned. There are of course inexhaustible records narrating the origins of particular wars, but war as a pattern of activity antedates by far the art of writing, and therefore the problem of its origins in the strict sense is insoluble. At most we can consider what might be the causes of its ubiquity.

The struggle for wealth, power and prestige is a constant feature of the life of humanity. Whether we like it or not the fact is that no society, no group however small, has ever been heard of where such a struggle would be altogether absent. Even associations of saintly ascetics are not quite immune from it. It is beyond any doubt that this universal trait of the social life of humans is due to the ineffaceable characteristics of human nature.

We might speculate on the problem of whether this tendency is related to an innate propensity for fighting, if this exists. In favour of the view that it does exist may be adduced the fact that little boys all over the world appear to be addicted to pugilism; even in environments where such behaviour is frowned upon. But the alternative explanation of this fact is equally plausible: namely, that scuffling is the only way in which the desire for power and

---

*On this point see S. Andreski, *Military Organization and Society*. London 1954: Routledge and Kegan Paul.

glory can be satisfied on the level of childish mentality. It is also probable that the feeling of belonging to a group, which appears to be indispensable to human happiness, does require some measure of antagonism to other groups. Nevertheless, even the assumption of innate pugnacity would not explain the existence of war because war means killing, and there is no evidence that there is in human beings an innate desire to kill their own kind; on the contrary, it seems that apart from a relatively few sadists most men dislike it. Usually, killing is done for the sake of other ends.

The natural propensities of men do not account for the systematic killing in which mankind indulges, because this practice is at variance with what goes on among other mammals. One of the chief reasons for this difference is the obvious circumstance which is seldom taken into account in the discussions of this problem: namely, the fact that human beings use weapons. Fisticuffs usually end with thrashings or the flight of the beaten; killing need not be a by-product of fighting, although it may follow it and be done on purpose. Furthermore, in such a situation a victor does not have to fear the vengeance of the weaker opponent. But this is not so if weapons are used, because then he who stabs or shoots first wins, and under such circumstances it is safest to kill one's enemies. Anyway, in all fighting where weapons are used some of the participants are likely to get killed. So we are justified in saying that the prevalence of killing within our species was made possible by the acquisition of culture.

War has been blamed on human nature, and it is perfectly true that if all men were kind and wise there would be no wars. It is clear that the capacity for cruelty is required for war, and the proneness to collective follies always facilitates wars and other kinds of social conflicts. Fortunately, however, there are reasons for doubting whether war is an absolutely necessary consequence of human nature being what it is. In every warlike polity (which means in an overwhelming majority of political formations of any kind) there are elaborate social arrangements which stimulate martial ardour by playing upon vanity, fear of contempt, sexual desire, filial and fraternal attachment, loyalty to the group and other sentiments. It seems reasonable to suppose that if there was an innate propensity to war-making, such a stimulation would be unnecessary. If human beings were in fact endowed with an innate proclivity for war, it would not be necessary to indoctrinate them with warlike virtues; and the mere fact that in so many societies past and present so much time has been devoted to such an indoctrination proves that there is no instinct for war.

Another important point is that in many nations for decades and even centuries only a very small minority of men took part in wars, so that the statistics of wars give a very exaggerated picture of the prevalence of bellicosity. For example: during the nearly three centuries between the death of Cromwell and 1914 Britain waged dozens of wars (or even hundreds if we include the colonial expeditions) but the soldiers who fought in battles constituted much less than 1 per cent of the population, and even they spent much more time in the barracks than on the battlefields. Nor is there much evidence that the majority thus condemned to a peaceful existence felt an irresistible desire for participating in wars, although it is true that many wars began with an outburst of collective enthusiasm.

It must not be forgotten how often direct compulsion had to be used not only in recruiting soldiers but also to make them fight. One of the masters of the craft—Frederick II of Prussia—enunciated the principle that a soldier must fear his officer more than the enemy; and according to Trotsky a soldier must be faced with the choice between a probable death if he advances and a certain death if he retreats.

If men had an innate propensity towards war, similar to their desire for food or sexual satisfaction, then there could be no instance of numerous nations remaining at peace for more than a generation. Nor can war be regarded as an inevitable consequence of national sovereignty because there are examples of sovereign states which have waged no wars for more than a century—these are Switzerland, Sweden, Norway and Denmark. One could say that with Switzerland, surrounded as it is by much more powerful neighbours—peacefulness is a matter of necessity rather than choice, but as far as the Scandinavian countries are concerned, it is clear that although they were too weak to attack their neighbours to the south, they could have fought among themselves, as many other small states did. There are a few other examples of peacefulness when a conquest would be very easy. The United States, for instance, could conquer Canada without much effort or fear of reprisals, and nevertheless, the Canadians have no fear of such a possibility. In spite of being exceptional, these examples do show that truly peaceful co-existence is possible.

It is often claimed that the remedy against war is to institute a world government but this view can be easily refuted. In the first place, political unification often merely means that instead of interstate wars, civil wars take place which can be just as bad or even worse. To mention one of very many possible examples: as soon as the Romans defeated their dangerous enemies, they started fighting among themselves, thus bringing the lands which they "pacified" into a much worse condition than they were in when they were divided into a multitude of independent and warring states. During the last hundred years the countries which waged fewest wars—Spain, Portugal and the republics of Latin America—had the longest record of internecine strife and revolutions. For this reason we cannot assume that we could eliminate bloodshed simply by instituting a world government because the outcome would depend on whether the sources of strife and violence would be eliminated.

Even more: it seems that there is an inverse connection between strenuous warfare and pretorianism. In Rome the civil wars began when Carthage—the last enemy who could threaten the very existence of the empire—had been destroyed.

In modern Europe the country which was most plagued by revolutions—Spain—did not take part in any major war since the times of Napoleon. What is even more telling is that it acquired this propensity only when it ceased to conquer and to send colonial expeditions. On the other hand, in Russia, which was nearly always at war and conquering, the army remained remarkably obedient. The Japanese, who remained confined to their islands nearly throughout their history by the over-whelming might of the Chinese empire, have an unrivalled record of civil wars. Latin America, where very few wars were fought, experienced more military revolts during the last century and a half than the rest of the world put together. The inverse connection between outward militancy and proneness to revolts, which the foregoing evidence suggests, is explained by the fact that external and civil wars are alternative releases of the pressure of population on resources.

It must be remembered that wars against rebels constituted, next to external wars, the chief occupation of governments throughout history. On the other hand, the only really peaceful area of the world—Scandinavia—has no supreme authority, the real cause of its peacefulness being that it is free from poverty and despotism. The same is true about internal peace: only countries where there is neither poverty nor despotism do not suffer from internal violence.

In conditions of misery, life, whether one's own or somebody else's, is not valued, and this facilitates greatly warlike propaganda. In an industrial society unemployment not only brings poverty but also breaks up social bonds and creates a large mass of uprooted men, whose frustrated desire for a place in society may lead them to favour measures of mass regimentation. Moreover, when there is not enough to satisfy the elementary needs of the population, the struggle for the good things of life becomes so bitter that democratic government, which always requires self-restraint and tolerance, becomes impossible, and despotism remains the only kind of government that can function at all. But absolute power creates the danger that a despot may push his country into war for the sake of satisfying his craving for power and glory.

The rulers who embark upon aggression at their own initiative are prompted chiefly by their desire for more power and glory—by the wish to be above their opposite numbers, and directing a war can be fun for a callous despot. Louis XIV—to mention one of innumerable possible examples—used to start a war whenever he was bored, without, of course, exposing himself to any dangers or privations. Unlike contemporary despots, he was quite frank about it. It follows that one condition of abolition of war is the elimination of situations which permit rulers to amuse themselves in this way at the expense of frightful suffering of their subjects: in other words, elimination of despotism. It is quite clear, unfortunately, that the existing despotic states cannot be transformed from outside, and our only hope is that they might gradually evolve into more humane forms of government.

The discrepancy between mechanical ingenuity and moral backwardness, which may very well prove fatal to mankind, is connected with the fact that whereas the technical level is fixed by the achievements of the most gifted inventors, the ethical level is determined less by the most benevolent of men than by their opposites, because of the way in which the processes of selection for positions of authority favour ruthless power-seekers. This seems to have always been so, but it is worth noting that the diminution of the role played by inheritance has brought no improvement in this respect. When thrones and dignities were hereditary they often fell to imbeciles or bloodthirsty madmen, but on occasions they came into the hands of benevolent men or women. When the posts of command are thrown open to competition, idlers and imbeciles have no chance, but neither have the gentle nor those with too many scruples, whilst bloodthirsty madmen are by no means excluded. A sociological generalization can be proposed that the more determined is the selection by the ability to manipulate men, the more ruthless and astute will be the rulers. To win a competitive prize one must desire it very strongly, and, therefore, nobody is likely to have power who does not crave it. For this reason, the issues on which the survival of the humanity depends will in all likelihood continue to be treated as gambits of power seeking.

Nuclear weapons might bring mankind to its doom or they might turn out to be a boon but they certainly prevent mankind from continuing on its normal course of customary brutality: men will have to treat each other better or they will all perish. By making war suicidal even for the rulers, the atomic weapons took away from them the opportunities of pushing others into carnage for the sake of their own amusement and glorification. Despotism still represents a great danger to peace because of the possibility that a madman might reach the position in which he could not be restrained from bringing everybody to destruction. A rational despot, however, cannot nowadays be excessively bellicose.

Countless covenants of peace and condemnations of war have proved to be of no avail against the evil propensities of the rulers, but there is a slight chance that the immediate danger to their lives might be more effective. It all hinges, however, on whether they will behave rationally.

Apart from general impediments to rational behaviour stemming from the apparently ineradicable waywardness of human nature, irrationality has been assiduously cultivated by various institutions, above all the armies. Inculcation of blind obedience and of readiness to die without asking why, and elevation of these habits to the status of the highest virtues, cannot fail to propagate irrationality. With the devaluation of the traditional martial virtues, rationality may come to be more appreciated. To be exact, this process has been going on for a very long time—in fact at least since the invention of firearms—but until now its pace has been exceedingly slow and there have been numerous relapses. In contrast, the change in this respect wrought by the advent of the atomic weapons promises to be quick and radical. It will probably diminish the chances of irrational types attaining positions of power, and thus reduce the risks of war. Bureaucratization also acts in the same direction, as it favours the ascent of calculating manipulators rather than of fiery demagogues or strong-arm men.*

As far as ordinary people are concerned, who have to endure all the sufferings, their most important motives in supporting aggression are: (1) collective frenzy or (2) simple obedience combined with the herd spirit, or (3) a sense of desperate frustration which makes them covet other people's goods, and welcome all adventures. Usually these factors are intertwined. The mass movements assume forms of collective mania chiefly in response to extreme frustration of elementary needs, including the need to have a secure place in the social order. Such frustration is most commonly the consequence of poverty, or at least of impoverishment in relation to customary standards. If that is so we need not be surprised that war was a permanent and universal institution for poverty was, everywhere—and still is in most parts of the world—a permanent condition of the great majority. Only in very recent times, and only in the few fortunate countries bordering the north Atlantic has grinding poverty become rare.

It is evident that some struggle must always go on in human societies; but only if it is a struggle for the necessities of life must it involve killing. But why, we are bound to ask, do men always fight for the necessities of life? Why can they not just share them and live quietly? The answer to this has been given by Malthus.

The theory of Malthus has the privilege of being one of the very few sociological generalizations which possess the degree of certainty equal to that of the laws of physics. Indeed, its truth is no less certain than that of the statement that the earth is round. Its essence is simple in the extreme. Human population is biologically capable of doubling itself every generation, that is to say, about every twenty-five years. This, says Malthus, cannot go on for long because there is a limit to the amount of food any given territory, or the earth as a whole, can produce. Something must happen, therefore, either to the birth-rate or to the death-rate. Either some biologically possible births are prevented, or people must live a shorter time than they are biologically capable of living. The factors which can

---

*On this point see S. Andreski, *Elements of Comparative Sociology*. London 1964: Weidenfeld and Nicolson.

lower the birth-rate—the preventive checks, as he calls them—
resolve themselves into two categories: vice and moral restraint.
He was mistaken as to the first because though prostitution and
venereal disease may produce sterility, promiscuity as such does
not. He was also too hopeful about the possible adoption of volun-
tary abstention, and did not envisage the modern practice of artificial
birth control. Nevertheless, the central idea is irrefutable: either
some births are prevented or deaths must be more frequent than is
biologically unavoidable. The factors which bring about the latter
result—the positive checks—are three: war, epidemics and starvation; and ultimately they are all consequences of misery, that is to
say, of the scarcity of food. And the only way of abolishing these
is the limitation of births. In other words, high birth-rate must, in
the long run, produce high death-rate, because population cannot
grow indefinitely.

A simple calculation shows that even if we started with a single
couple the biological powers of procreation would be sufficient to
cover the whole surface of the earth with human bodies in a few
millennia. Even at the present rate of growth, which is certainly
below the biologically possible maximum, the population of the
world would become so large before the lapse of two thousand years
that there would be no room for people to stand on. Even if people
inhabited many-storied houses covering the whole surface of the
globe, even floating on the oceans, and lived on pills produced by
direct transformation of solar energy, even then the end would be
in sight because the increase in the mass of our globe would cause
it to crash into the sun. The views of Malthus have been and are
being misrepresented because his theory touches the sex taboo,
presents unpalatable truth useless for demagogic purposes, and in
addition reveals the inevitable consequences of demographic expansionism, so alluring to group megalomania, and so dear to leaders
lusting for power.

Until the introduction of modern contraceptive practices the
importance of preventive checks was slight. The effects of their
prevalence in some restricted areas would be outweighed by numerous births elsewhere. Killing one another could not have remained
one of the chief occupations of men if there had been no surplus of
men available. The natural tendency of the population to grow
beyond the means of subsistence assured the permanence of bloody
struggles. Although sheer hunger has driven men into battle much
more often than people brought up in opulent countries imagine,
the growth of population can produce war or some other form of
strife long before the point of starvation is reached: the mere drop
from the customary standard of living may generate bellicose
pulsions. Moreover, intensive warfare may keep the standard of
living well above the subsistence level. Malthus, commenting on
the relative opulence of the Kirghiz, remarks: "He who determines
to be rich or die cannot long live poor" (Essay, p. 76). Many

primitive tribes began to experience permanent starvation only after the pacification by the colonial governments.

The recognition of this fact enables us to advance a hypothesis about the origin of war. As nothing of the sort exists among the mammals this institution must be the creation of culture. It probably came into existence when the advance in material culture enabled man to defend himself better against the beasts which preyed on him, and thus to disturb the natural balance which keeps the numbers of any species stationary in the long run. After the beasts had been subdued, another man became the chief obstacle in the search for food; and mutual killing began. A similar view has been expressed by a Chinese philosopher Han Fei-tzu (*circa* fifth century B.C.) (quoted by J. J. L. Duyvendak in the introduction to his translation of *The Book of Lord Shang*, London 1928, p. 104) according to whom: "The men of old did not till the field, but the fruits of plants and trees were sufficient for food. Nor did the women weave, for the furs of birds and animals were enough for clothing. Without working there was enough to live, there were few people and plenty of supplies, and therefore the people did not quarrel. So neither large rewards nor heavy punishments were used, but the people governed themselves. But nowadays people do not consider a family of five children as large, and each child having again five children, before the death of the grandfather, there may be twenty-five grandchildren. The result is that there are many people and few supplies, that one has to work hard for a meagre return. So the people fall to quarrelling and though rewards may be doubled and punishments heaped up, one does not get away from disorder."

The remedies of signing treaties of eternal peace, convening congresses and preaching condemnation of wars, have been tried innumerable times and without much effect. They may be needed but in themselves are clearly insufficient. Elimination of poverty has not yet been tried except in very restricted areas where it had, in fact, the result of instilling into people a pacific disposition.

Given the propensities of human nature, the tendency of the population to grow beyond the resources has insured the ubiquity of wars, although not every single instance of war had this factor as an immediate cause. Wars might cease to be a permanent feature of social life only after the restoration of the demographic balance whose disappearance at an early stage of cultural development made them inevitable.

POSSIBLE SUBSTITUTES FOR WAR

By

ANTHONY STORR

116 *Harley Street, London, England*

THE psychiatrist who, like myself, specializes in psychotherapy, must necessarily feel ill at ease when speaking to such an audience as this, especially when his place on the programme is such that he has followed so many scientists whose opinions are backed by experiment and verification.

The doctor who seeks to help the individual human being is always at a disadvantage compared with the biologist, the anthropologist, or the historian. For his conclusions are bound to be limited by the human material with which he deals. His conception of human nature is closely circumscribed by the consulting room, and, although the view from a Harley Street window may take in the activities of a Dr. Ward or a Miss Keeler in the neighbouring mews, it cannot comprehend the wider vistas which unfold themselves before those whose concern is with the destinies of nations, of races, or of species. Remember then that what I have to say is limited because my experience is limited, and that in discussing the natural history of aggression, my observations are based upon my experience of treating a relatively small number of human beings who may themselves be unrepresentative of even Western society in general.

My subject is entitled "Possible Substitutes for War", and this title itself implies that war has not always been regarded as wholly evil. For if a thing is totally bad, we should surely seek simply to abolish it, rather than to look for substitutes for it. The very fact that we might need substitutes for war implies that war satisfies a need in our human nature, and thus has something valuable about it. We don't look for substitutes for cholera or the plague, although I suppose certain groups of persons might regard contraception in the same light, or even as a worse evil than these epidemics. Until the invention of nuclear weapons, however, there can be no doubt that war satisfied deeply felt needs, and this is why men have been so reluctant to abandon it. If we are to discuss possible substitutes for war, it is important first to examine the satisfactions which war used to provide.

One of these satisfactions was certainly an increased sense of identity with others. American research into human reactions to disaster has shown that, under extreme threat, human beings cling more closely together. Distinctions of class, of age, of status, all tend to disappear. Faced with a common enemy, whether this be flood or fire or human opponent, we become brothers in a way which never obtains in ordinary life. It is a great thing to have an enemy, for it is only then that we discover our neighbour; only then that we can transcend the barriers of class, of education or of creed which generally divide us, and which descend once more when external danger ceases to threaten us. The comradeship of war, the fact that, under conditions of stress, our capacity for identification with our fellows is increased, has been one reason for the continued popularity of war. There can be few people who do not recall something of the increased warmth they both showed towards and received from their fellow men after exposure to some such common danger as a night's bombing of London; and there are many who look back to the days of the blitz with nostalgia, as is evidenced by the eagerness with which, even twenty years after, they are prepared to recall those sleepless nights and smoking dawns. Hand in hand with this increased feeling of companionship, of identity with the group, goes a diminished sense of individual responsibility. Every psychiatrist is familiar with cases of men who broke down under stress of peace, because they were unable to resume personal responsibility for their lives or to take decisions which, during war, had generally been taken for them. In a democratic society we tend to assume that every adult individual is capable of independence and rational decision. But, in wartime, innumerable individuals are thankful to abandon the burden of conscious choice, to submerge their individuality in a crowd, and to take their orders from above. To be fed, clothed, and delivered from immediate anxiety is such a relief to many characters that these advantages amply compensate them for the loss of liberty which is their inevitable accompaniment.

Nor is this relief confined to the weak or to the neurotic: decision-making is a burden to all of us, which is why we tend to give high financial rewards to the decision-makers in our society. In wartime, life is simplified for everyone, for the collective decision has been taken that the enemy must be defeated; and all other decisions and values are subsidiary to this one. Those people, therefore, who have some difficulty in finding any overruling purpose to which to devote their lives and who are unsatisfied by the mundane incentives which motivate the average person, find an almost religious satisfaction in devoting themselves to one main objective, and in orientating their lives in submission to the single wartime aim of victory.

The psychological advantages of a feeling of group solidarity, of relief from personal responsibility, and of the incentive given by a sense of purpose merit further discussion, but this conference is principally concerned with aggression, and there can be little doubt that, in the past, an important function of war was to provide an opportunity for the apparently justifiable discharge of those aggressive impulses which seem so inescapable a part of human nature.

Elsewhere I have tried to define what I mean by aggression, and find it very difficult. At the risk of repetition, I must briefly summarize my argument. Like most psychotherapists nowadays, to whatever school they may belong, I cannot accept Freud's idea of a "death instinct". Freud's conception of aggression was that it was primarily self-destructive; an instinct which, to quote his own words, was "trying to bring living matter back into an inorganic condition". The aggressiveness which men show towards the external world was, in Freud's view, a secondary phenomenon. The death instinct was the primary urge, a kind of personification of the second law of thermodynamics. Although decay and death are certainly our lot, and although, as Eddington puts it, time's arrow cannot be reversed, I cannot believe in an instinct which is self-destructive. Entropy constantly increases, but whatever the forces are within us which lead to our final dissolution, they are not to be subsumed under the same heading as the instincts which serve to preserve us or to encourage us to reproduce. Surely the very concept of instinct is of a pattern of behaviour which is of some value to the organism in question.

Nor is it possible to accept the idea that man's aggression is merely a response to frustration. No one doubts that frustration increases aggressiveness: you have only to try and drive a car in London at 5.30 p.m. on any weekday evening to discover this. But to imagine that, if only we had all had ideally loving parents and the serenest of possible childhoods we would not be aggressive creatures, is to be totally unrealistic about human nature.

Throughout history men have had a vision of the millennium; a condition in which perfect peace would prevail, men would agree with each other, and we should all be splendidly co-operative, creative and free. This vision can be found in Greek mythology, in Ovid, in Isaiah, and even in Bertrand Russell. Men think that a world without war would be a world without aggression; and envisage a future in which we should all reach undreamed-of heights of prosperity and achievement, under the beneficent care of a single world government.

Such visions are based on the idea that we can somehow get rid of our aggression. If only, these prophets allege, inequality between nations was abolished, or capitalism overthrown, or Esperanto universally spoken, or birth control everywhere adopted—then, at last, we should be able to live at peace with one another, and our true nature, pacific, gentle and loving, become universally manifest.

The idea that we can get rid of aggression seems to me to be nonsense. Surely everything we know of the behaviour of men in groups contradicts this conception. Innumerable attempts have been made to found communities in which there would be no cause for strife—but strife always breaks in; and where it is least expected, it is usually most destructive. My favourite example is the psychoanalytic movement. No sooner had Freud established himself when Adler broke away and then Jung. Later, the Freudian school was split in two by the heterodoxy of Melanie Klein, and the Jungian group has been similarly riven. Those of you in academic life will know of many comparable examples. Man's aggression is more than a response to frustration—it is an attempt to assert himself as an individual, to separate himself from the herd, to find his own identity.

As you will understand, the conception of aggression which I am advancing is one which lays stress upon its positive aspects. My observation of individuals leads me to suppose that aggression only becomes really dangerous when it is suppressed or disowned. The man who is able to assert himself is seldom vicious; it is the weak who are most likely to stab one in the back.

This positive aspect of aggression is seldom emphasized. Owing to an accident of history, Freud, who has had more influence than any other individual upon man's view of his own nature, did not admit the existence of a separate aggressive drive until fairly late in his life, and then found it so difficult to fit into his scheme that he was led into the blind alley of the death instinct conception. Other psychologists, however, notably Alfred Adler, have always recognized that a striving for superiority or urge for power, or desire for self-assertion, exists, and common sense demands that some such drive be recognized as of equal importance with the sexual instinct.

It is generally admitted that the further back into infancy one pursues the phantasies of children, the more aggression does one find, and it is impossible to believe that the whole of this aggressive potential springs from frustration at the breast. Even the most lovingly reared children generally go through a phase of rebellion at about the age of three, in which they assert their own individuality in powerfully aggressive terms. Adolescents repeat this pattern at a later stage. Indeed, adolescents need to rebel, and when there is nothing to rebel against, invent imaginary figures upon whom to vent their wrath. The notable increase in juvenile crime in the last twenty years may actually be connected with the lessening of external frustration. If parents cannot be treated as scapegoats, aggression finds other objects to attack.

Moreover, it is important to realize that no new discovery would ever be made if men were not intolerant of the old and violently assertive of the new. Aggression and creation march hand in hand and, as Bernard Berensen once put it, "Genius is the capacity for productive reaction against one's training".

In considering war and the opportunity which it provided for expressing the aggressive side of our nature, most writers have either fallen into the trap of millenniary pacifism or else exalted war with a kind of schoolboy jingoism which I find utterly repulsive. War is a great and pressing evil which we must get rid of, but it is no use supposing that we can change human nature into something pacific and gentle. For, in our efforts to realize our full potential, struggle and opposition are absolutely necessary. If enemies do not exist, we promptly invent them, as anyone who has served on a committee must know. Our mistake is to think that anything is achieved by destroying our enemies. On the contrary, we ought to struggle to preserve them.

The affluent society cushions us against hunger, against disease, and against destruction, and in doing so, deprives us of any opportunity to test ourselves to the limit, to struggle or to die. No wonder the old-fashioned kind of war was popular. For, in our humdrum passage from our well-sprung perambulators to our decorous coffins, what opportunities have we for heroism, for self-sacrifice, or for identifying ourselves with causes which transcend our petty struggles for recognition, for status, or for dominance in the human pecking order? Until nuclear weapons finally precluded heroism, war did provide a field in which men realized potentialities of courage and endurance which seldom come their way in peace time. To wait until senile decrepitude puts an end to one's protracted plush existence is not necessarily an agreeable prospect, and many natures only find fulfilment in circumstances where they are exposed to risk or at least discomfort.

The human tendency to welcome difficulties and dangers is a very interesting one. To my mind it is not fully explained by the psycho-analytic theory of masochism. Of course there are people who torture and punish themselves, consciously or unconsciously, for past offences. Of course there are people who can never allow themselves any pleasure, and who make even the smallest task into a difficult, painful examination which they never pass. On the other hand, not every task which a man may set himself falls into this category and it cannot be assumed that to welcome a certain amount of difficulty and danger is invariably pathological. To attempt the North Face of the Eiger may be a piece of masochistic folly, but not everyone who enjoys physical exertion followed by relaxation is attempting to bolster a shaky masculinity. "Strength", said Leonardo da Vinci, "is born of constraint and dies in freedom" and without a certain constraint, how is a man to discover his own strength? It seems to me that an attitude to life which takes some pleasure in overcoming obstacles or facing risks is preferable to one in which everything unpleasant is avoided and the easiest path invariably preferred, and, in the past, war has afforded men opportunities for stretching themselves to the limit, thus not only proving their strength, but evoking potentialities perhaps undreamed of in peaceful conditions.

Human potentialities which are unused tend to cause trouble to their owner. The buried talent does not lie quietly in the ground, but sets up subterranean disturbances which manifest themselves in the form of anxiety and other symptoms. Freud showed us how the repression of sexuality could lead to neurotic symptoms which have far-reaching effects on the health and happiness of the whole being. To deny expression to so important a part of human nature is to run the risk that nature will protest.

In the same way it seems probable that the denial or repression of our aggressive drives is liable to cause disharmony within ourselves, however desirable it may be that we should get rid of them. Judging from the popularity of violence on the cinema screen and television, the eagerness with which we watch boxing or wrestling, and the delight with which we read of murder, it seems certain that, automatically and inevitably, we are constantly seeking opportunities for the vicarious expression of aggressive drives. Can it be that our form of civilization is at fault? Erich Fromm has pointed out that the highest rates of suicide and alcoholism are to be found in countries which are generally considered the most democratic, peaceful and prosperous. Denmark, Switzerland, Finland, Sweden and the U.S.A. head the list. Suicide is obviously a turning in of aggression against the self, and alcoholism is equally an expression of the way in which men destroy themselves. In this country, over 5,000 people a year commit suicide, whilst 30,000 attempt it; and although we do not commit many murders, the threefold increase in our prison population since 1938 and the racial disturbances in Notting Hill and elsewhere, surely attest the presence of violent destructive impulses which we contain within us only with difficulty. In war, these impulses used to find an acceptable channel for discharge. They can do so no longer except in wars between nations who do not possess nuclear weapons. Any satisfaction which some megalomaniac statesmen might obtain from the despatch of a nuclear missile is likely to be swiftly curtailed by his own annihilation; and although another Hitler might prefer to destroy the world and himself together, he will not thereby be providing us with an outlet for our own aggressive drives.

It seems to me just possible that we shall succeed in avoiding the holocaust; a view which has received support from the events of the Cuban crisis. But the outlawing of nuclear war, or even the abolition of war altogether, does not solve the problem of our own aggressiveness. In some ways it makes it more difficult, and that is why we ought to consider possible substitutes for war.

In a recent book, Professor Rapoport of the University of Michigan, who works at the Center for Research on Conflict Resolution, has discussed the various ways in which mathematical theory can be applied to the study of human conflict. He calls his book *Fights, Games and Debates*, and he advances the hope that our fights may be changed into games and our games into debates. His viewpoint has the signal virtue of recognizing that the alternative to war is not necessarily peace. Clausewitz defined war as "The continuation of policy by other means." Our only hope is that we can continue war by other means than the primitive one of killing each other.

This is not an impossible task, for it has been solved by other members of the animal kingdom. As Professor Eckhard Hess wrote recently of fighting between members of the same species: "Actions that injure the opponent have been removed to the end of the sequence of fighting behaviour by raising the threshold for its release to a very high level. This resulted in the development of tournaments with a very small likelihood of actual bodily harm, a development which has clear survival value to the species, since fighting behaviour will maintain its function of spacing out members of the same species without causing injury to species members."

It may seem stupidly naïve to think that we can substitute ritual struggles for war; but in my view this has already happened. It is not so long ago that we found our enemies from north of the border a serious menace against whom we sent punitive expeditions. Now we defeat them at Twickenham, or are ourselves defeated. The struggle remains, but the form of it is different. I am not so naïve as to imagine that serious conflicts of interest between sovereign states can be settled by football matches or gladiatorial encounters. But I do believe that serious conflicts of interest between sovereign states are not now the real problem, except, perhaps in those parts of the world which are grossly over-populated. The days when great powers might come into conflict because they were greedily competing for rich slices of Africa are surely over. What we have to deal with now are the problems of ideological conflicts—in other words, with psychology even more than with economics. Although we have not yet solved the problem of the underdeveloped countries, we do know more or less what to do about them, and it seems unlikely that nuclear war will break out as a form of conflict between the haves and have-nots, more especially if we can prevent the spread of nuclear weapons.

Ideological conflicts will go on so long as human nature remains as it is; it is the problem of resolving these without recourse to destructive violence which we have to deal with. I was recently taken to task for defending the vast sums spent on the space race on the grounds that it might be serving the function of a ritual conflict between East and West. Those who believe that conflict can be abolished would rather see the money spent on welfare, and I sympathize with their desire. But, so long as sovereign states exist there will be competitive struggles between them. The desire for prestige and power is stronger than the desire to see everyone cared for. And, in considering human nature, it must be taken into account. Do you remember how at the time of Cuba the newspapers were much concerned with Mr. Kruschev's pride? Was he going to be able to climb down without too much loss of prestige or not?

It is absurd to think that millions of lives may depend upon whether a single individual's self-esteem is damaged, but such is human nature. If I am right in thinking that the space race serves a valuable function, we should not grudge expenditure on it.

I do not believe that ideological conflicts can be solved by the deliberate substitution of alternatives. But, because of man's innate aggression, these alternatives arise automatically if conflict in the form of war is impossible. There will always be plenty of ways in which countries can compete, whether it be in the space race, in education, in technology, or even in welfare. We ought to encourage competition in these fields as much as we possibly can.

But there is one vital step which has to be taken if we are to ensure that ritual and other forms of struggle are to become substitutes for war. This step is what Professor Rapoport has called the "assumption of similarity". In playing a game, we generally suppose that our opponent is a man like ourselves, who will think in roughly the same way, strike at the same objectives, and make the same sort of choices. In war, propaganda plays upon the paranoid tendency, latent in all of us, which enables us to regard other members of our species as totally different. It is not difficult to convince people that if a man has a skin of a different colour and professes a different faith, he is so utterly alien that he deserves to be destroyed. One may not kill one's neighbour; but that other man, the enemy, deserves nothing but death. For is he not a raper of women, a torturer of children, a bomber of civilians?—but I had better not go on. Thinking of the bombing of Dresden, of the Suez fiasco, of Hola, of Cyprus, and even of Aden, it is well for me to stop. For what I want to destroy in my enemy is what I cannot stomach in myself, and to kill him is to commit suicide. It is only when we can fully realize this truth that we can learn to value our enemy, and learn to fight him without destroying him. "Any man's death diminishes me, because I am involved in mankind: and therefore never send to know for whom the bell tolls; it tolls for thee."

THE NATURE OF AGGRESSION AS REVEALED IN THE ATOMIC AGE

By

JOHN BURTON

University College, London, England

Introduction

THE circumstances of the post-war world seem to be exposing the nature of conflict. In the days of conventional weapons, situations of apparent aggression tended to develop quickly and to promote immediate political and military responses, and consequently their causes could not currently be analysed. History is liberally scattered with records of wars which commenced with what appeared at the time to be unprovoked aggression. In our memory are the aggressions of Italy, Germany and Japan. What led to aggression was not clearly perceived at the time; and in any event it would not have been politically expedient to contradict official and popular explanations which accompanied a country's war effort.

In the nuclear age, in which firstly there is an overwhelming power of destruction the use of which no state can readily contemplate, and in which secondly, there is a world forum at which large numbers of independent peoples can freely express themselves, time and opportunity are available for analysis of situations of aggression as they develop. In the pre-SEATO days of disturbance in the territories which were formerly French Indo-China, the United States had a virtual monopoly of nuclear power. In 1953 Mr. Dulles threatened overwhelming force at a time and place of American choosing if Communist aggression continued. He was employing the orthodox tactics of power politics of the pre-nuclear age, but with nuclear weapons. There was a widespread reaction even in the United States, and hesitation in implementing such a grave threat gave opportunity for some objective assessments of Nationalism as a movement quite separate from Communism. Once thoughtful discussion and debate had taken place in press, parliaments and on popular platforms, the threat could not be implemented, at least without inviting the active hostility of Asian, African and important sections of Western public opinion. The restraint was due not just to the consequence of the use of nuclear weapons—far

more importantly it was due to the grave doubts raised about the
merits of the United States case. The prolonged tug-of-war between
existing and opposing regimes in South East Asia has continued
ever since, and there are now appearing, after some ten years of
public debate, grave doubts in Western circles as to the wisdom
and justice of supporting unpopular and repressive regimes, and
blaming local opposition to them upon "communist aggression".
If it had not been for the power of modern weapons, and the
hesitations which enabled debate, Mr. Dulles might have been able
to act; China would have been destroyed, and movements dubbed
communist would have been repressed in South East Asia; history
would have recorded the episode as another example of meeting
aggression—whereas thanks to nuclear weapons and to world public
debate there are at least some doubts about the guilt of the accused.

This was the position when the United States had a virtual
monopoly of nuclear power. The development of a mutual deterrence
now causes even greater hesitation, and occasions even more important delays, thus giving opportunities of world assessment of
complicated situations. Perhaps Suez will make for the historian a
turning point in world affairs as important as Cuba; in such cases in
the pre-nuclear age, invasion could have been completed quickly and
effectively by the power whose interests seemed to be threatened. The
mutual deterrent of the thermo-nuclear age has provided opportunity
for reflection, just at a time when the interests and opinions of smaller
nations are a matter of great relevance in power politics. Law,
justice, strategic consequences, morality, the role of vested interests,
are all matters now widely debated in respect of any crisis situation.
The consequence is that a clearer vision as to what constitutes
aggression is now being obtained.

What is being revealed by this nuclear-age slow-motion picture
of aggression appears to be quite different from the orthodox and
popular notion. I wish to argue in this paper, firstly that there is
no theoretical foundation for the notion of aggression by sovereign
states; and secondly, that even if there were, there is currently no
evidence of aggression amongst sovereign states.

Aggressiveness

THE notion of aggressiveness in animals may finally be shown to
be valid; however, it should not escape attention that in the present
state of our knowledge we have no conclusive evidence of this. The
pecking-hen is a most contented bird once placed in a single cage
from which it can enjoy the company of other female machines
without fearing them, and the aggressive cow in the milking yard
undergoes what appears to be a change in character once it is
polled. But even though biologists can show aggressiveness in lower
forms of life to be a prime motivation, human aggressiveness is not
thereby established. There may be a continuum in cortical evolution,
but this does not argue against effective cortical dominance of

behaviour at a certain stage. Indeed, whatever may be the case with animals, psychologists seem generally to agree that "there is no direct physiological basis for aggression, although the blocked, frustrated or deprived organism can be counted on to show the physiological changes accompanying emotion. . . . One cannot cite man's inherent aggressiveness as a factor that makes war inevitable" (Sanford, 1961). Aggressiveness is described and understood by psychologists in terms of frustration, fear, displacement, scapegoating, rationalization, projection, compensation, identification, and a host of other relevant concepts, and this seems to indicate that aggressiveness is an emergent or dependent state of mind.

This academic conception of aggression as a secondary or derived motivation does not prevent aggressiveness being treated by law, and by society generally, as a primary one for which the individual himself is responsible. We still endeavour to control and to suppress aggression by the individual without regard to environmental causation. Just as vagabonds were once hounded as lazy people, and not considered to be the product of a system which included unemployment, so aggressive people are still an object of social condemnation, and subject to laws designed to suppress them.

This gap between academic theory and social practice, which exists within a society, is very small when compared with the gap existing between the same theory and practice within the international community. We did not stop to consider the degree to which Western nations were directly and indirectly responsible for Italian, German and Japanese aggressions, and all the atrocities associated with them.

Not only is the gap between theory and practice greater in our approach to international aggression, but the consequences are greater. The gaoling or execution of the aggressive individual does not destroy society. But in the international field, any attempt to repress apparent aggressiveness, as an alternative to the early removal of the underlying causes of the aggression, is of vital concern to the whole of civilization. At best there results a temporary peace, and at worst there is world war. We are, however, prepared to leave this gap unbridged; it is more expedient in a system of power politics for a state to create an image of unprovoked aggression than to indulge in a little self-criticism of its own policies.

A Logical Difficulty

So far I have been arguing there is no positive evidence of aggressiveness as a prime motivation in the individual, and by analogy, there is no reason for assuming a nation is aggressive. Now I wish to suggest that even though the popular notion of aggressiveness in the individual as a prime motivation were valid, it still could not logically be argued that states were aggressive.

While certain behavioural aspects of international affairs are obvious, there is no valid application of terms and concepts developed in a closed society to relations between states. In recent years there have been many dangerous extensions into the international community of concepts developed in relation to the closed society. International affairs have come to be attractive as an "interdisciplinary" study. Terminology which is precise in, and relevant to a particular discipline, has infiltrated into discussion of international affairs, and we are fast building up a series of convenient images of the world to suit the convenience of psychologists, psychiatrists, educationalists, biologists, physicists and others, and we are analyzing and prescribing for defects revealed, believing that we are dealing with the real world.

One of the most common—and as I hope to show, one of the most dangerous—images is that of an international society in which nations each have the attributes of persons within a community. Abnormal psychology, games-theory, value judgements and moral responses, then appear to be immediately relevant to international studies. In reality the nation-state is not of this order; if there must be an analogy (and I see no reason why there should be any), then it would be at least as appropriate to use mechanics or electronics as sociology. It is only by describing the world system of power politics as it operates that there can be any understanding of it; and then it becomes clear why mentally healthy leaders appear to respond abnormally in the international system, why moral men take immoral decisions, why mild and humble leading-elite appear aggressive. It is true that nations are led by humans, and that these people are subject to certain pressures from other humans, and it is therefore true that there are important problems associated with perception and understanding of the policies and motives of others; but to argue some continuum in the development from a family, to a tribe, to a community, to an international society, is false. Families may have some characteristics and responses which can be described in terms appropriate to its members, but the state and its machinery of government cannot be given these same psychological attributes.

Any theory which postulates the continuous development of social organization from primitive forms to an international society, leads logically to world government as a final goal to be sought. If in fact there is no continuum, the goal may be unattainable, even in theory, and energies will have been wrongly directed, leading to failure and disaster, in addition to academic and popular disillusionment and desperation. Indeed the dangers of a false approach are greater than mere disillusionment. When the biologists and the psychologists assert that there are aggressive tendencies amongst individuals within nations, and imply that nation-states tend to act aggressively, then they are encouraging every state to have an expectation of aggression, even though there is no discernible enemy. The defence policy of the state will tend to produce just the results it seeks to avoid, and the ultimate responsibility for this could be that of the intellectual in society. One wonders to what extent the philosophers of the past have been directly responsible for peace-through-strength ideas, and the whole notion of national independence being a function of defence capability.

It is difficult even for the academic to divorce himself from popular notions. For example, Hans Morgenthau (1960), despite references in one passage to the elements of fear and frustration in aggression, has difficulty in bridging this gap between scientific and popular conceptions of aggression. He is prepared to assert that it is possible to predict on the basis of the past because of "those elemental bio-psychological drives by which in turn society is created." He continues, "The essence of international politics is identical with its domestic counterpart." On this basis every responsible government is fully justified in taking extreme and provocative defence measures. Studies of International Relations, for example, *Power Politics* by Professor Schwarzenberger (1964), which are based on the power approach, seem to assume an aggressive nature of Man and the State, though they do not always argue these assumptions. Professor Waltz (1959) in his useful book *Man, the State and War*, has effectively, I think, demolished several of these pre-conceived notions, in particular the single-cause approaches which suggest that man or the state is responsible for war. Professor Claude (1961) has by careful analysis, destroyed any reason for seeking power-balances, collective security, or world government, as our haven. I suspect that if more work were done along the same lines it would be found that modern political thought, East and West, is full of implied assumptions, false premises and causes and cures derived from folk-lore of the past, which have been handed down without much question for hundreds of years.

Aggression and Change

These comments should not be taken as implying that social and natural sciences have no contribution to make to International Relations, and to the study of power politics. "Aggression" is a term most commonly used by those who are satisfied with the *status quo*, and who resist any attempt to upset the existing order. International Relations studies have tended throughout the years to concentrate upon the maintenance of an existing order; balance of power, collective security and world government, all tend to act in favour of those who are satisfied. The machinery for peaceful change is not something which has received adequate attention. If one were to assume that every apparently aggressive action were prompted by some awareness of injustice or some sense of frustration, and if one were to look for the cause of this, aggression would appear in a different light. What is required of the social scientist is more study of change; the perception of change, the different effects upon interested parties of change introduced by objective agents, such as the weather, as compared with subjective agents such as states or monopolies; the means of making passive adjustments to change so that the adjustment will not lead to further aggressive responses by others; international machinery to ensure that perception of change is not distorted into the perception of a deliberate act of aggression. The inability of the West, and in particular of the United States of America, to accept and to adjust to changes in political institutions in other countries, and in particular in the People's Republic of China, the responses of China and the image it has of the United States, and the further non-passive responses of the United States, have created a situation of major concern—where objectively there is no call for such tension. Research is needed into misunderstanding and failure of communication, and into a wide variety of matters not conventionally within the established discipline of International Relations. But there are limits to the usefulness of such research. Part of the data of international studies must be good and bad men, good and bad institutions, and many other static features of an international system, in the same sense that geography, the weather, population growth, and such matters must be taken as fixed.

The Real World

So far I have argued only that we are by no means certain that aggression is a prime motivation in animals or men, and even if we were, it would not necessarily follow that aggressiveness can be attributed to nation-states. This is only negative reasoning—all I have said is that there is no proof that aggression exists. It is most important, I would say vital in the literal sense, to determine positively whether or not international aggressiveness exists. If it can be shown that some of the basic assumptions on which policy rests are invalid, for instance if it can be shown that states are not inherently aggressive in their endeavours to secure their interests, then we can reasonably give thought to programmes and policies not tied to this assumption—programmes and policies which might avoid the competitive development of defences and the ultimate employment of nuclear warfare. The orthodox approach to international affairs, on which our foreign policies are currently based, would be turned upside down if fear, frustration and deprivation were popularly and officially accepted as the prime motivations of defence policies, rather than some inevitable aggressive urge. The seemingly aggressive policies of states would then be perceived, not as a struggle for power for its own sake, but as a power-struggle designed to avoid the consequences of aggressiveness by others which has unjustifiably been assumed to exist.

Let us turn to the real world, where aggression can now be observed in the slow-motion of the nuclear stalemate. I wish to draw my examples from Asia and South East Asia, which is a current centre of apparent aggression. In this area traditional expectations of aggression have led to policies which have appeared to be aggressive to both Communist and Western leadership. There have been actual confrontations, and expectations of aggression have become self-supporting. In Vietnam and Thailand, in Formosa and Korea, Western support for unpopular and sometimes repressive regimes has had the appearance to the Chinese of a deliberate encirclement, and aggressive intents have been deduced from frequent, though unofficial and irresponsible, statements coming out of the United States. Chinese responses in each of these areas have in turn appeared to be aggressive, and have seemed to justify Western policies.

Once unpopular governments are maintained by foreign support in the context of the United States confrontation with Communism, any local oppositions, even genuine national ones, can conveniently be labelled subversive, and dealt with as such. This has happened both in Communist and in Western-dominated nations. It is by this process that there has developed the appearance of active Communist aggression in South East Asia, even when there is no tangible evidence of aggression. Admittedly the existence of internal unrest due to a feudal land-tenure system, and to extremes of privilege, does not prove that foreign subversion is absent. But it can be said that any government which lacks popular support, and whose continuation in office is of strategic value to a major power, is bound to argue that internal threats to its security are inspired by a foreign power. It can also be said that intervention by a foreign power will be interpreted by a nation in the opposing power-bloc as aggressive in intent. It is the duty of any government in the system of power politics to prepare for the worst, and to take counter-measures against the type of military encirclement which the West has imposed on China.

The element of fear in Chinese policies is understandable—most countries in the area, for diverse reasons, seem to wish to contain if not to damage China. After ten years of isolation from world councils, the element of frustration is also inevitable. China, like Japan before the war, having tried every means of breaking through the barriers to normal political and economic intercourse, will, if the isolation is maintained, have little option but to aggress; but this will not prove that China is an aggressive country, or has been forced by population pressures to expand, or has been brought into conflict by revolutionary leadership. It will prove only that Western responses to change in China have promoted fear and frustration in China.

It is not appropriate here to examine in detail either the Korean conflict or the Indian-Chinese border dispute. I wish to comment only that in neither case do the facts that are now available to Western observers give support to any notion of unprovoked aggressiveness or of expansionism on the part of China. In both cases expectations of Chinese aggression, arising out of false perception, out of processes of projection, and out of a high state of propaganda-tension, gave rise to policies and actions which provoked Chinese responses that could readily be labelled as aggressive. In both cases domestic political considerations of a most pressing nature in the countries confronting China—the United States and India— were relevant to the policies which preceded tense relations with China.

Nonalignment and Aggression

In this role-reversal exercise I may have over-stated the case for China and against the West, in my attempt to put a viewpoint. Support for this view that aggression is not a prime motivation in international relationships has emerged as an unintended effect of nonalignment. The nonaligned nations comprise a variety of political systems including capitalist, feudal and communist. Some, like Burma and Cambodia, happen to be on or near the borders of China, yet they seem to consider themselves more secure in relation to China than in relation to some of their neighbours. Thailand and Vietnam, on the other hand, even though not as close to China, are aligned with a great power and allow that power to establish bases, and depend upon it for their security. They fear Chinese aggression more than the nonaligned Burma and Cambodia. Non-alignment seems to be demonstrating that security may be possible, even for a small country on the border of a major power, provided firstly that it has internal political support, and secondly that there is no threat from it to that neighbouring power by reason of foreign bases for use by an opposing major power. In this way nonalignment seems to have shown that apparent aggression is a policy based on false perception, upon fear of aggression, and not on some innate or inevitable aggressive instinct or desire for power on the part of sovereign states. It seems to show, moreover, that the type of system, whether it be communist of capitalist is not important in power politics: a state is not aggressive in a primary sense, regardless of its internal institutions. This is not the occasion to speak about nonalignment as such, but it is relevant to observe that avoidance of military alliances may be a strategic policy more in accord both with political reality and with our academic knowledge of the nature of aggression, than the traditional policies of alliances which consistently throughout history have ultimately produced the results they sought to avoid.

A Scientific Approach to Peace

Publicity has recently been given to scientific approaches to peace, and with special references to the social disciplines. There is little doubt that almost every branch of learning has some contribution to make to the wide study of peaceful relations amongst sovereign states. Nevertheless, over-enthusiasm in finding a place for a particular discipline could be destructive of peace. I have referred to the defence preparations which flow from the propagation of the idea that aggression by man and by states is inevitable. The scientific contribution of the biologist might be a claim that he has no contribution, that the cause of war is not directly related to aggressiveness, and that in fact he has no reason to believe that aggressiveness is an attribute of a sovereign state. The extension of the findings of biology and psychology into the international relationship is probably false; but as an analogy it could be useful to point out that in animals and in man, aggressiveness is a non-passive response to the perception of a threat, or to the experience of a frustration.   Political leaders of states who accuse other states of being aggressive, would then know where the responsibility for aggression finally lies.

References
Claude, I. L.   1961.   *Power and International Relations.*   Random House.
Morgenthau, H.   1960.   *Politics Among Nations.*   Knopf.
Sanford, F. H.   1961.   *Psychology—A Scientific Study of Man.*   Wadsworth Publishing Co. Inc.
Schwarzenberger, G.   1964.   *Power Politics.*   Stevens.
Waltz, K. N.   1959.   *Man, the State and War.*   Columbia.

LORENZ: I do not deny that governments may cause wars without being motivated by anything comparable to the instinctive drive of intraspecific aggression. Business considerations have obviously proved a quite sufficient motive. But the point is, no politician ever could make men really fight, if it were not for very archaic, instinctive reactions of the crowd on which to play. One of these reactions is that of so-called enthusiasm. A detailed description of it is given in my book. The German word *"Begeisterung"* implies that the spirit has descended on a man in this mental state, the Greek word "enthusiasm" even makes out that it is a god that has taken possession of him, both of which shows plainly what exceptional subjective phenomena are inherent to the response in question. Objectively, it is less godlike, but strongly reminiscent of the behaviour patterns which chimps show when they are working up to the social defence of the horde. Shoulders squared, chin thrust forward and the hairs on the upper back and the outside of the forearms bristling—subjectively a slight shiver—chimp and man alike prepare to risk their life in the interests of their community. With the predictability of a reflex, this reaction can be released by a strictly defined stimulus situation. First of all, the community to which the individual belongs and/or, in man, values representing it, must appear to be threatened by an outward enemy. The family, the nation, old school ties, a football club or the integrity of scientific ethics may represent the values which, when jeopardized, elicit enthusiastic defence. I intentionally mention things which do appear as values to myself together with others that do not, in order to demonstrate the unselectiveness of the response. The role of the "enemy" may be played by an even larger variety of concrete things and abstract conceptions. "The" tyrants, bourgeois, exploiters, bolshevics, huns, jews, boches, etc., have proved equally good dummies to release the response under discussion. An inspiring leader—with whom even the most anti-fascist regimes by an even larger variety of concrete things and abstract conceptions. joining in the same enthusiasm, serve as additional stimulation. Rhythmic noise produced in chorus is even observed in chimps as means to work up to communal attack, and everybody knows the inspiring effect of "'varsity songs, march music and national anthems.

Please do not misconstrue my meaning. It is not *enthusiasm* that is bad, but its miscarrying. It is not *aggression* or, for that matter, any other instinct that is evil, but the disturbance of its function wrought by the cultural change in human sociology, by changes too quick for the slow, phylogenetic adaptation of instincts. Aggression, and its special communal form of "enthusiasm" is as indispensable to the social structure of mankind as any other human instinct, and more indispensable than any others for the attainment of high, specifically human goals. A man incapable of enthusiasm is an emotional cripple and no good to humanity. One who is susceptible to it, but unaware of the reflex-like compulsion it entails, is a danger to humanity, because he is an easy prey to cynical demagogues who release fighting enthusiasm much as we do in our experimental animals, and who, at present times, seem to be the only men alive who have at least a practical working knowledge of human instincts, using it for their own, anti-humanitarian ends. Honest politicians, working for the best of humanity, ought to take a leaf out of the demagogues' book and use the knowledge underlying the war-monger's methods to prevent wars. The point of our present symposium on the Natural History of Aggression is that the latter might add appreciably to that knowledge.

BERG: Have you discounted learning? I think we all agree that aggression is innate in so far as we all have a mechanism for showing aggression. Monkeys are innately afraid of snakes, but can learn not to fear them. It has been said that the amount of aggressive material on television shows our need for the expression of aggressive drives, but recent work has shown that these aggressive displays on films of children make children behave aggressively. I am referring to Bandura's work. The most recent "Utopia" has been written by a psychologist, Professor Skinner of Harvard. He shows how people could live together peacefully by appropriate education.

STORR: Professor Norman Cohn in his book "The Pursuit of the Millennium" demonstrates that there is a regular pattern in the emergence of paranoid leaders such as Hitler? Such people arise on a basis of frustration and misery because they promise in the future a millennium of peace and plenty, and because they provide an enemy such as the Jews or anti-Christ against whom the frustrated aggression of the people they lead can be directed.

SOLOMON: It is quite clear that wars have provided outlets for aggression, also that people's aggressive tendencies have been exploited in order to enlist their support for wars that have already broken out. But is human aggressiveness an important cause of war? This is quite a different matter. It seems important that historians, sociologists and psychologists should combine in an enquiry into the causes of war, to clarify the part played by aggressive impulses (and by fear), as distinct from the calculations of governments about possible economic or other advantages. The assessment would presumably be quite different for the present day and for earlier periods, even within the present century.

RUSSELL: It seems important to bring to the attention of the symposium the recent work of Professor Harry F. Harlow and his associates in the United States. For, in the last couple of years, they have provided cogent evidence that a high level of aggressiveness in primates is the product of upbringing. We must first distinguish between two things; rage, on the one hand, and on the other the sort of intense destructive aggressiveness we can observe in human crime, civil strife, or war.

The mechanism of rage is usually called by ethologists the attack drive. It is innately present in most higher animals, including ourselves, though in several species it is known to mature late, certainly later than fear. It is simply a mechanism for reacting to frustration of needs, including the need to do things. In some lower animal species, natural selection has caused this mechanism to be active at a high level over long periods in the life of the individual: it is then no longer exactly related to the amount of real frustration present. This may happen, as Professor Lorenz told us, because defence against predators or parasites demands an extremely active attack drive. We then have a species with innately intense aggressiveness, such as the gannet, with unfortunate consequences for social life, which natural selection will alleviate by other devices. The rage mechanism is controlled in the part of the brain called the hypothalamus, a structure common to many animals. But in higher mammals, a special circuit is provided to bring this mechanism under the control of the cerebral cortex, which is known to be the basis of intelligence in man. This means that in ourselves rage could be simply a signal of the presence of frustration, in principle under intelligent control. Where intelligence is unable to function freely, the mechanism of rage can be influenced by conditioning processes, and cease to be under intelligent control. From the anatomical facts, known for a decade or so, we might expect intense aggressiveness in primates to be a product of culture and upbringing.

This expectation is confirmed by the experiments of Harlow and his colleagues. They reared rhesus monkeys in isolation from their mothers, but with access to each other, in a sort of orphan society free of adult influence. The orphans established relations with each other a little less rapidly and smoothly than similar groups allowed access to their mother as well. But by the time they grew up, the orphans were behaviourally healthy monkeys, with normal sexual and exploratory behaviour, and normally moderate levels of rage. Some young monkeys, however, were reared in isolation, not only from their mothers, but also from each other. These grew up to be seriously behaviourally disturbed. They somewhat resembled human schizophrenic patients. When given the opportunity later, they showed no positive social responses of any kind. They sat staring in their cages, biting themselves if a human approached. Their sexual behaviour was grossly impaired. But a few females thus reared were finally impregnated by exceptionally patient and persistent normal males. These females in due course produced young, and may then be described as "motherless mothers".

The behaviour of motherless mothers to their own young was appalling and inhuman (or unsimian). They showed no positive response or attention. The young monkeys made unceasing attempts to obtain bodily contact with their mothers, only to be thrown aside or crushed to the ground, as if they were rubbish or parasites. Like the orphans considered earlier, the young monkeys did have access to each other, and they grew up with some capacity for social behaviour. But they had clearly been subjected to intolerable frustration in early life. As they grew up, they showed *more aggression* than any of the other groups studied, and sometimes seemed to resemble human juvenile delinquents.

Obviously all Harlow's monkeys, like all human beings, must have had rage mechanisms. But intense aggressiveness, abnormal for the species, only appeared in those subjected to rearing by a "bad" mother. And we must remember that these "bad" mothers were themselves so on account of the way they had been reared. It is clear that a high level of aggressiveness in a primate is the product of cultural tradition.

We know from Japanese work that tradition in monkeys is largely transmitted by maternal upbringing. In man, of course, culture is transmitted not only by parents but also, especially in adolescence, by initiation, indoctrination and other social pressures, or, positively, by education. All these factors may combine to produce intense aggressiveness in human individuals: that is, levels of attack drive unrelated to real current frustration. If we explore these factors, we may hope to eliminate intense aggressiveness from human social behaviour, leaving only a normal rage function, as a valuable signal of real frustration. Nor can we any longer be complacent about the failure of our societies to remove real frustrations and solve economic, social and educational problems; for we cannot now perpetuate the old excuse that human beings are innately intensely aggressive and need to be disciplined.

FREEMAN: I invite the last speaker to indicate in a reply of one word only whether he considers Harlow's researches can be interpreted as meaning that there is no sexual drive in the rhesus monkey.

RUSSELL: No.

ANABEL WILLIAMS-ELLIS: There has been one curious omission from these four otherwise admirable discussion sessions. No one has said so much as a word about the Doctrine of the Class War. Yet this doctrine is what one of the two powerful protagonists in the present dangerous confrontation, believes (or anyhow declares) to be the real historical foundation of human aggression—the class struggle and its most modern manifestation, imperialism. I, and most of us here, may well believe that to attribute so much to a single cause is an oversimplification, or perhaps (much more dangerous) a rationalization.

All the same it remains a doctrine believed (or accepted) by most of the inhabitants of two of the currently most powerful and intellectually potent nations, Russia and China. It is the foundation of a set of doctrines whose inevitability and ubiquity is asserted by one side—the Marxists— and denied by the other. It is thus (nominally at least) the *causus belli* of the cold war, and could be that of an atomic conflict. It has perhaps been natural for the naturalists to ignore it. But what about the sociologists and our historian?

HARRISON: Dr. Burton has suggested that a body such as a state or nation cannot by its nature react aggressively, but surely any decision of a state is ultimately the decision of a particular person holding a responsible office. While such individuals may be capable of rational and abstract reasoning they also possess normal innate emotional reactions; and we know that where reasoning and emotional reactions conflict the latter will override reasoning, and such an individual will be as capable of an aggressive reaction as any other. If these people believe that the action which they take is supported by the majority of their fellows this may lead to a war which is as much an individual aggressive reaction as any which we have considered.

BURTON: A distinction has to be made between men as actors and states as actors. The head of a state or a politician cannot act as a person. He is subject to all numbers of pressures and consults a variety of advisers. He may act, in practice, in ways quite contrary to his own judgment or wishes, and he may act as the head of a state in ways quite incompatible with his own private personality. The point I wish to underline is that states act, in their view, responsibly in relation to the interests of the state. What appears to be aggression to the other party appears to them to be no more than the exercise of their rights in defence of their interests or in legitimate pursuit of their interests. The difference between a war of defence and a war of aggression is the point from which the war is seen.

COHN: Does Dr. Burton consider that war would have broken out in 1939 if Germany had not at that time been governed by a paranoid megalomaniac?

BURTON: War broke out in 1939 not because of the particular character of the leader of Germany. The fact that that leader was there was due to circumstances which dated back for many years and the actual conflict situation was in existence long before 1939. When states are frustrated in achieving their objectives, as for example in the case of Japan which required raw materials and markets for its development, then leaders are put into office who are prepared to pursue these objectives by means other than negotiation. It is not helpful in any analysis of conflict to commence at the point of actual military warfare.

CROFT: What is the possibility of a deranged individual in a position of power initiating an atomic war?

BURTON: There are on record a few cases of attempts to commence atomic warfare by deranged people. However, the system of checks is said to be foolproof and this, of course, is a problem of which technicians are constantly aware and the checks are constantly improved. My view would be that the dangers of accidental or irresponsible nuclear war are declining.